MW01630875

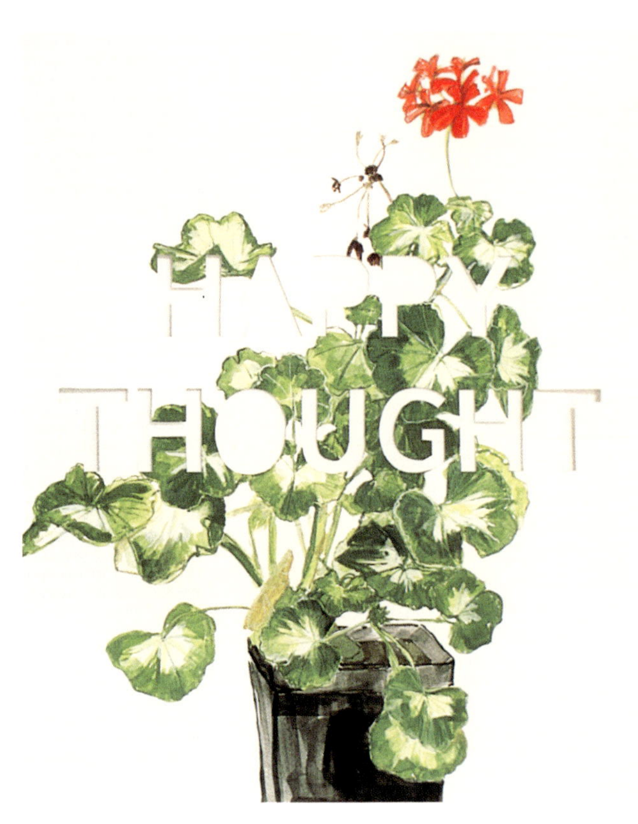
HAPPY
THOUGHT

Roy McMakin loves wordplay. Although he is not a writer and does not indulge in poetry (at least as traditionally practiced), the slight manipulation of letters within words, or words within sentences, tantalizes him, mostly for the surprises and revelations that arise when fixed meanings slip their tethers and run rampant into new territories. In his art and design, McMakin sets up similar getaways, allowing his seemingly familiar objects to slowly pull away from their well-worn referents and take on fresh guises. For the most part, McMakin's vocabulary is drawn from the domestic realm, where safety, regularity, stability, and shelter rule, making his disruptions all the more poignant and affecting.

As the title of this book and exhibition suggests, **function**, **representation**, **ornamentation**, **decoration**, and **adulation** are all examined in McMakin's work as components of domestic life that have historically found themselves in opposing camps. His career too has been split between art and design, balancing as many differences as similarities. Metaphor and reality are constantly intertwined in his practice: **Can a door be both functional and ornamental?** Can it ever shed its utilitarian status and become purely aesthetic? What to make of an image of a door? Is hanging a door akin to wearing a necklace?

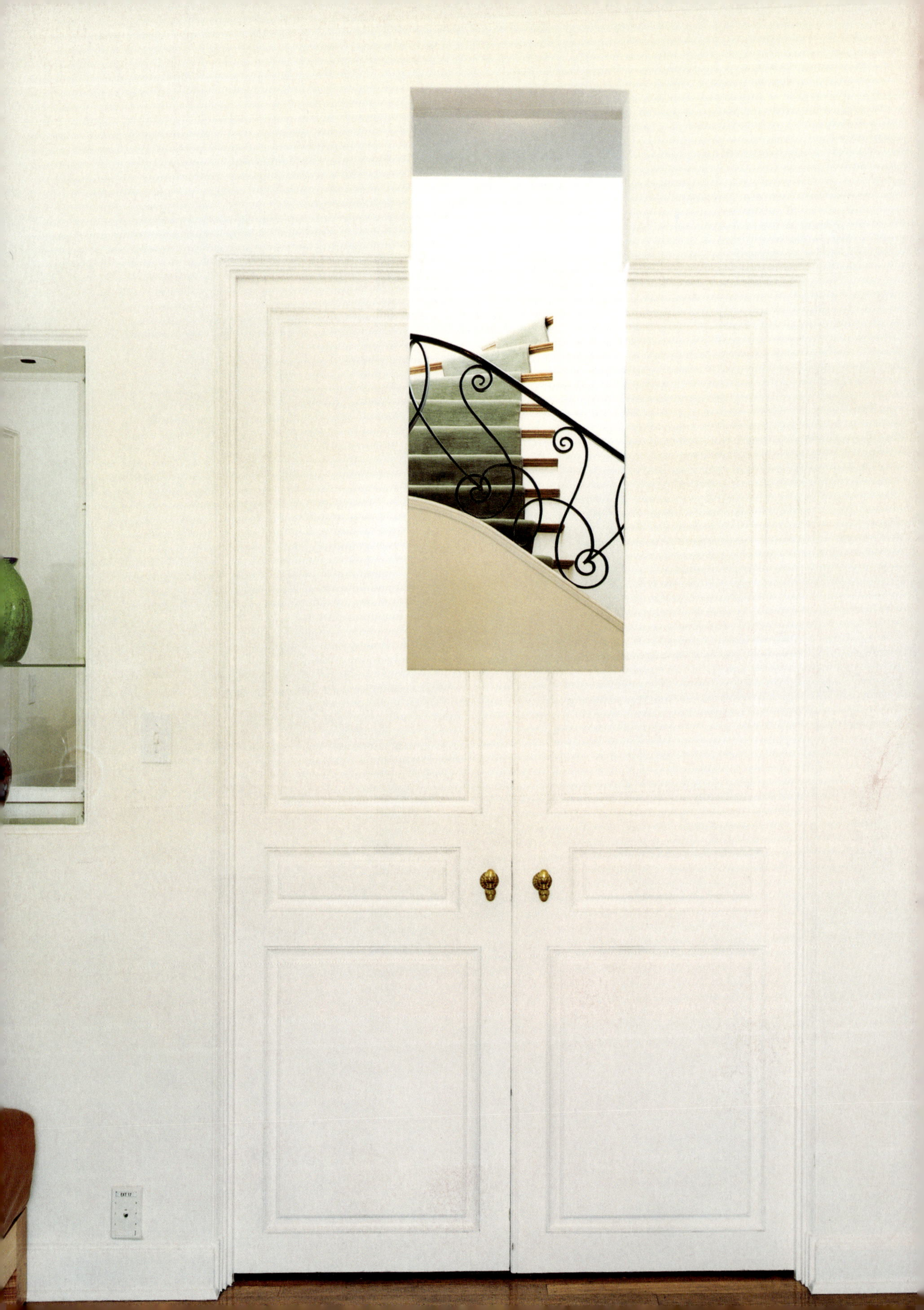

ROY McMAKIN

a Door Meant *as* Adornment

Michael Darling

THE MUSEUM OF CONTEMPORARY ART
LOS ANGELES

Poetic interconnections between the words "adore," "adornment," "ornament," and "store" make them ripe for McMakin's gamesmanship and allow him to conflate disparate concepts and uncover surprising connections. For McMakin, furniture and domestic architecture have long offered a framework within which to enact these contextual corruptions, bringing poetic play home to where it naturally and comfortably encounters the body on a daily basis. As he has said, "There is something...about setting up systems and then having to break up the system because some bit of reality, of life, gets in the way.... That delights me and interests me to no end."[1] The slight shift of letters and spacing, the glitch in the system, that transforms "a door" to "adore" is a metaphor for his dual practice as a problem-solving designer and problem-creating artist — a dichotomy that he has come to actively court and that sets him apart from so many others who veer into one realm or the other.

McMakin was an art student during the late 1970s and early 80s at the University of California at San Diego (UCSD), a hotbed of artistic engagement with the everyday. From Allan Kaprow, inventor of the Happening, to domestic conceptualist Eleanor Antin, environmental-art pioneers Helen Mayer Harrison and Newton Harrison, film critic and painter Manny Farber, and painter Patricia Patterson, the UCSD faculty espoused boundary-breaking, experimental approaches to art-making. Early on, McMakin identified architecture and furniture as ready vehicles for his own conceptual and phenomenological explorations of shifts in meaning. A 1979 untitled sculpture, for instance, featured a wooden table with a pane of glass sitting askew on its surface and a glass of water precariously balanced on top — a delicious dichotomy of opaque and transparent structures. One year later, the artist turned to performance art to investigate style-derived structure in furniture. In *Love in a Charles Eames Chair* (1980), performed at the San Diego alternative space Sushi, classic modern design and its orderly aspirations as a rigid system slowly deteriorated as the chaos of life, embodied by the actors and their dialogue, took over. In 1982, also at Sushi,

McMakin turned to installation as a way to address similar issues, building what looked to be a full-scale domestic dwelling within the gallery space. As viewers entered *A House*, the impermanent, propped-up walls and disturbingly non-functional passageways prompted reflections upon the assumed requirements of a true house.

Around the same time, McMakin also brought domestic objects to bear on the practice of painting, seeking to draw painting off the wall and into the functional sphere of the everyday. In an untitled piece from 1981, for instance, McMakin built a Shaker-style end table whose simple lines and slightly unusual details (such as a tabletop that extends further than one would expect) anticipated his work as a practicing furniture designer. On the drawer face, the artist painted a serene seascape in the manner of John Frederick Kensett that cannot escape the intrusive functionality of its context. A knob sits contentedly on the horizon line and the painting's frame consists of legs and cabinetry that threaten to disrupt the pure aesthetic moment. In this early work one finds an unexpected take on the classic figure/ground relationship, as painting and table are locked in a dynamic push and pull to assert their place in the hierarchy of visual phenomena. For McMakin, the battle between figure and ground, between an object and its surroundings, is made especially stark when furniture is pulled from the functional backdrop of our lives and pushed to the forefront of aesthetic appreciation or attention.

Such poetic recontextualization leads to more philosophical questions as well, forcing viewers to consider the value judgments they make on a daily basis about the objects around them. The 1982 work *Landscape, Table, Box* performs a similar operation; here McMakin placed a 1950s-style coffee table against a wall so that it abutted a pastoral landscape painting's lower edge. Both the landscape and the table share a similar hue, drawing the space of the painting out into the room, while the eponymous box, a found object sitting on the table, bears an expressively painted surface so that it too is stuck in the gray zone between the aesthetic space of the painting

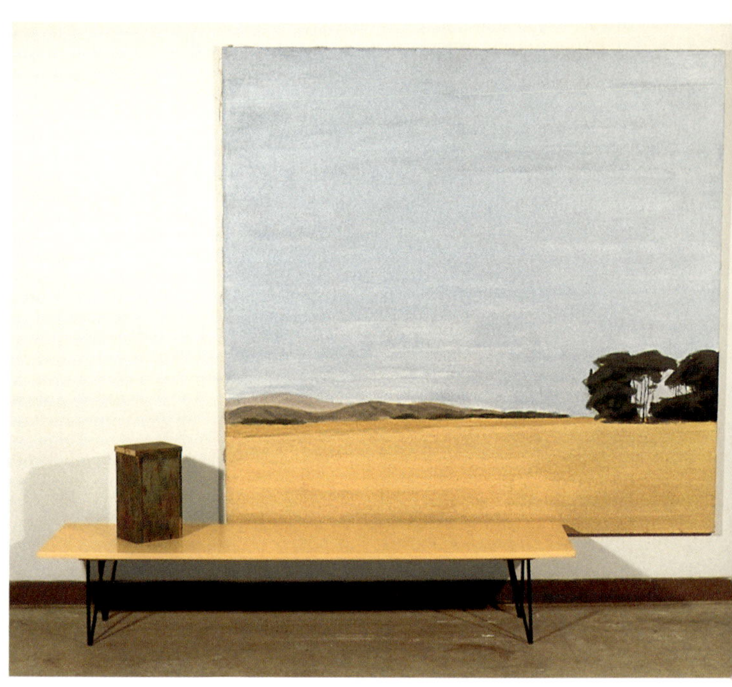

LANDSCAPE, TABLE, BOX, 1982
acrylic on canvas with mixed media
84 x 72 x 24 inches

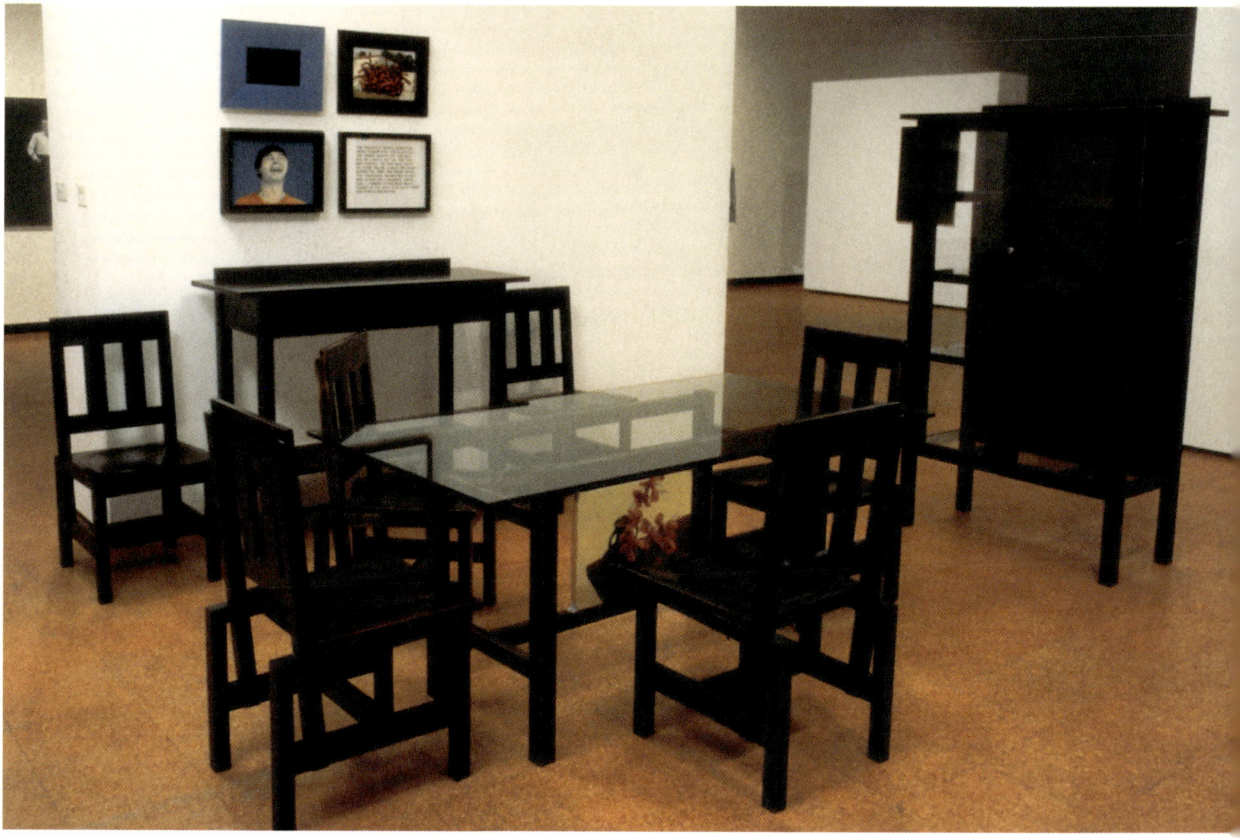

A DINING ROOM SET, 1983
acrylic and pigmented varnish on maple and glass
dimensions variable

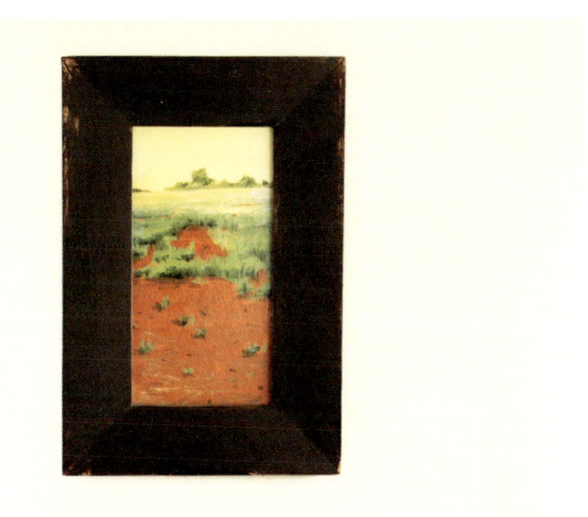

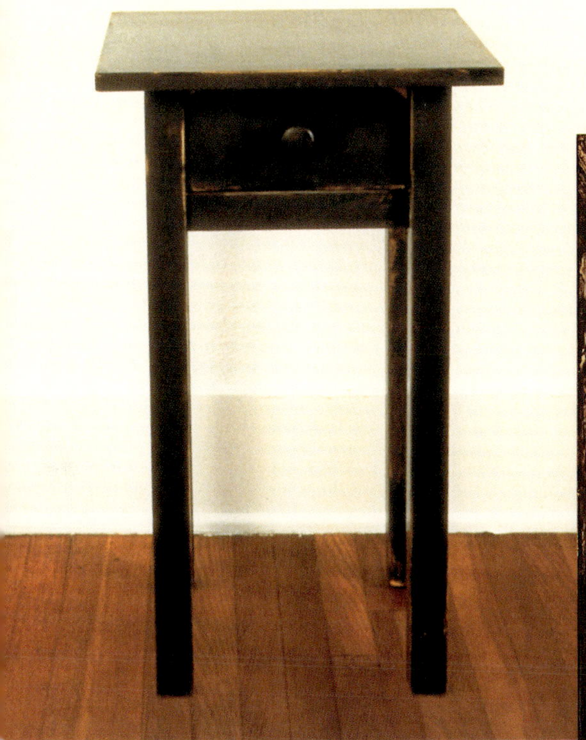

from **ROY MELVIN'S DEATH**, 1994

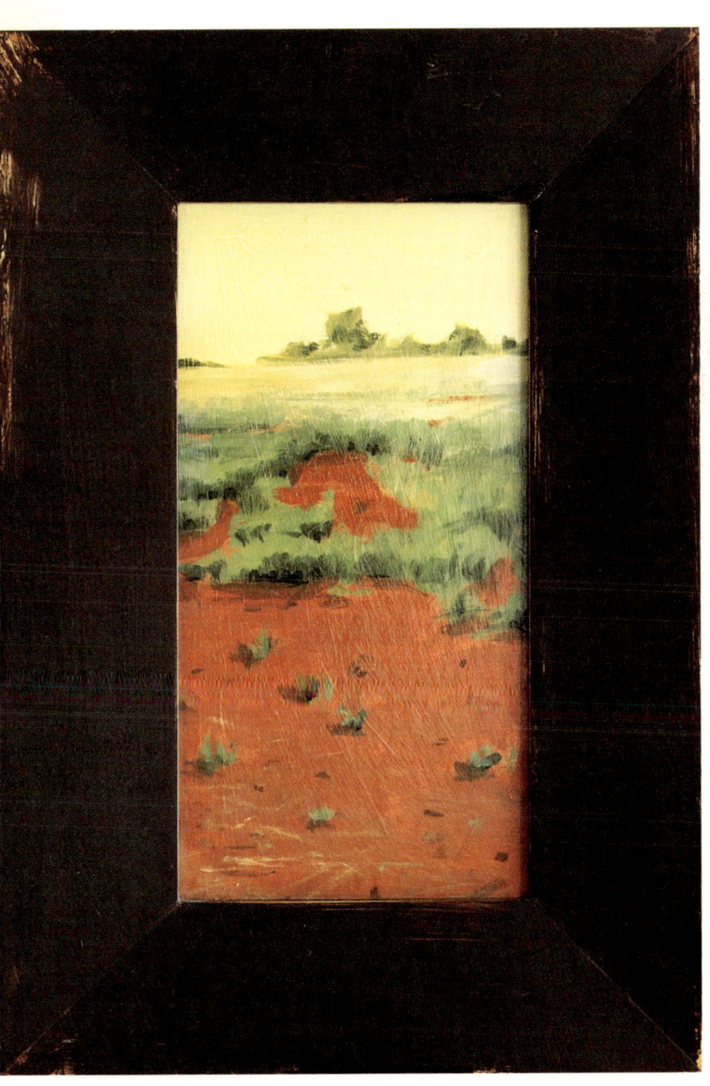

and the functional space of the room. In many ways, such an exercise in boundary-blurring harkens back to Pablo Picasso's incorporation of chair caning in his painting, or the conflations of life and art one finds in the early works of Jasper Johns or Robert Rauschenberg, such as *According to What* (1964) by the former and *Pilgrim* (1960) by the latter. It also coincides with the theatrical deployment of furniture found in New York artist Scott Burton's work from around this time and relates to work Jim Isermann was beginning to make in Los Angeles. Where Burton's work turned towards blending monumental, modernist sculpture with furniture and Isermann went on to investigate the degradation of high modern design into mass-produced kitsch, McMakin continued to engage issues of domesticity, memory, and the conventions of furniture construction.

In *A Dining Room Set* (1983), for instance, McMakin set out to make a sculptural group look antique through dark finishes and a simplified, almost craftsmanlike construction in order to inspire a sense of nostalgia and loss. The dark, brushed-on surfaces of the furniture and openwork nature of its construction, coupled with the use of glass in the dining table and china cabinet, heighten the awareness of each structural part — a quality that is a hallmark of McMakin's subsequent commercial furniture work. The china cabinet's exposed sides, glass shelves, and bottom, in particular, are later taken up in numerous iterations, while the side chairs, with their rigorously geometric slats and voids, similarly become sites of compositional interest for the artist.

The death of McMakin's grandfather, who he frequently and fondly visited in Oklahoma as a child, inspired a series of six paintings that again collapse painting and furniture so as to make furniture a more provocative and evocative object in one's life while bringing painting more actively into the realm of everyday existence. Collectively titled *Roy Melvin's Death* (1984), the series features loosely painted landscapes in heavy black and brown frames whose surfaces are similarly expressive and match the small side tables with which they are paired. Recalling the oft-seen placement of a mirror above a hall table in a domestic setting, the landscapes become insistent reflections that ask viewers to connect the scenes with their own memories.

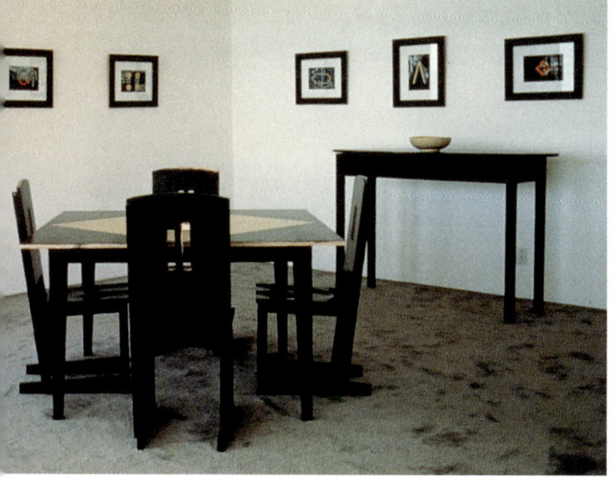

Such painterly furniture was revisited again in an important exhibition in 1985 at the Museum of Contemporary Art San Diego at La Jolla (MCASD, then known as the La Jolla Museum of Contemporary Art), where McMakin's *An Informal Dining Room Set* (1985) comprised equally dark, hand-finished furniture arranged as if in a home. A china cabinet, sideboard, dining table, and four chairs were laid out rather conventionally in the room, except for the fact that the china cabinet was placed in front of one of the gallery's large windows, partially blocking the view to the ocean. A triangular perforation in the cabinet allowed a glimpse of the view beyond, and adjacent windows featured geometric framing devices affixed directly to the glass. A suite of photographs in the gallery offered views of a house that were likewise strategically framed by ellipses, diamonds, rectangles, and other shapes. The photographs were taken in a home designed by proto-modernist architect Irving Gill, the same architect who built the house now occupied by the MCASD. In effect, McMakin attempted to reinscribe the scale and feeling of Gill's domestic environment back onto the clean white box of the contemporary art space.

Indeed, Gill was known for his own brand of white architecture, often stripped to spare rectilinear volumes punctured by unfussy windows and simple arches. However, McMakin came to appreciate the humane qualities and sensitive details of Gill's houses after living in one from 1982 to 1985. McMakin lived in Gill's Mary Cossitt Residence (1906), whose exterior is a

AN INFORMAL DINING ROOM SET, 1985
enamel on maple and photographs
dimensions variable
installation view, La Jolla Museum of Contemporary Art
La Jolla, California, 1985

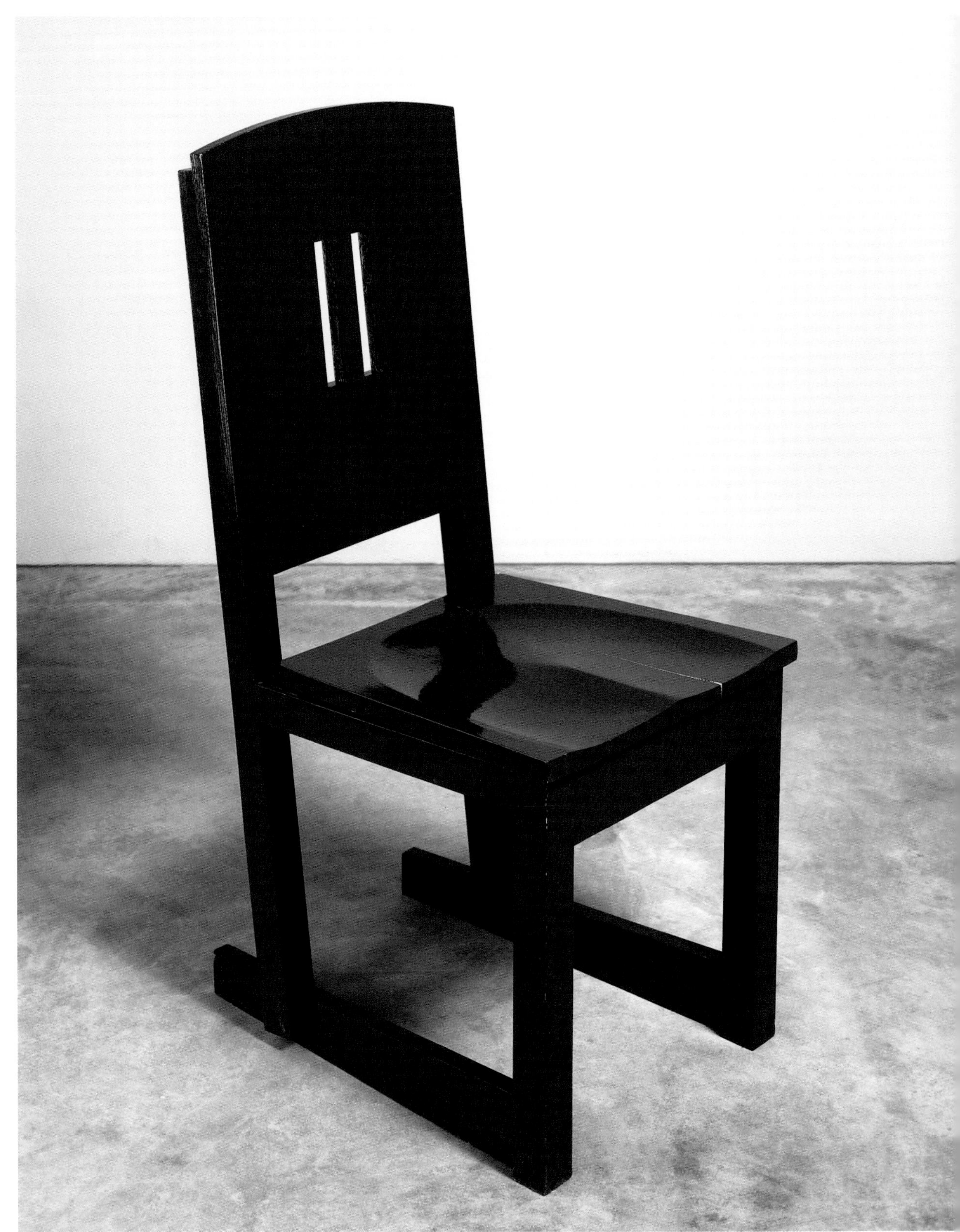

chair from **AN INFORMAL DINING ROOM SET**, 1985

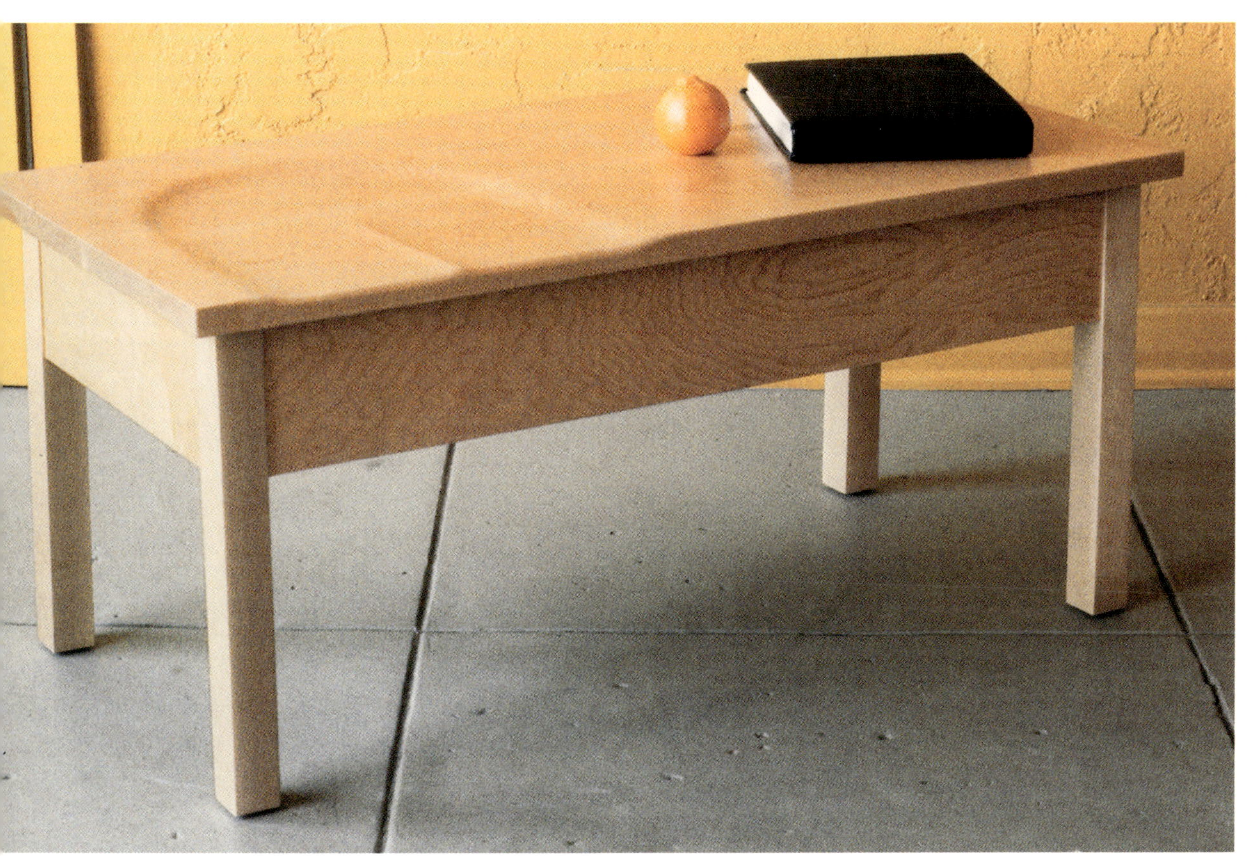

CAUDAL BENCH, 1989

mix of cubic and Wrightian Prairie styles while its interior is woodsy and craftsmanlike. The young artist was highly influenced by Gill's stripped-down aesthetic approach, where forms were reduced to their essentials. It wasn't minimalism for minimalism's sake that appealed to McMakin but the way Gill's buildings quietly choreograph one's life, and how function and form conduct a gentle dialogue with one another. In Gill, McMakin found the collapse of figure and ground that so intrigued him: exteriors press inside just as the architecture exerts itself as a frame on its surroundings. The detailing of Gill's buildings also presented a platform for the enhancement of everyday activities so that the ordinary was often allowed to appear extraordinary. For example, the subtle swell at the center of a fireplace mantle in some Gill houses announces a logical spot for the placement of a vase or other decorative item, creating a subtle decorative flourish while also satisfying a functional requirement for extra depth. Much of McMakin's subsequent furniture and architecture similarly foregrounds use and function. Gill's place in McMakin's aesthetic development led the artist to purchase and restore another Gill building, the 1917 Morgan House in Los Angeles, which precipitated a fateful move to that city in 1987.

In the MCASD installation, McMakin's aspiration to Gill's marriage of compositional clarity and human comfort was visible, especially in the dining chairs. Here, the image of a chair was simultaneously enforced and undermined by the strong sense of geometric abstraction employed by the artist, where solids and voids were emphasized by dark surfaces within a white room. The anatomically mimetic seat of the chair brought the emphasis back around to functional use and later became a Gill-inspired signifier in pieces like his Caudal Bench (1989). Also present in this installation was an interest in gracefully dissonant geometric forms, as shown in the sideboard that featured an ovoid wood top with a rectangular base. These later formed the basis for an entire body of work.

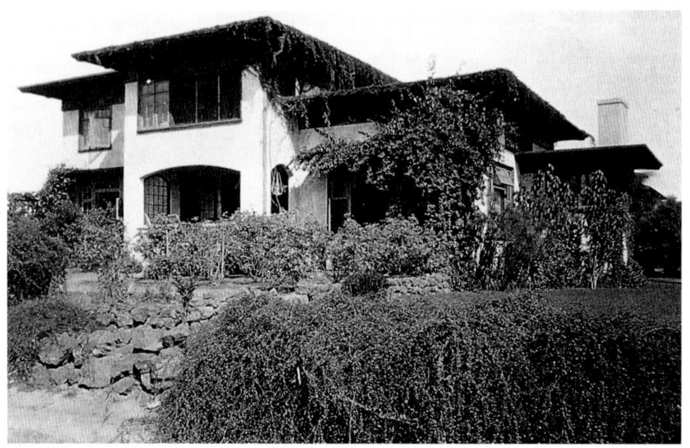

Irving Gill with W. S. Hebbard
MARY COSSITT RESIDENCE #4
SAN DIEGO, 1906

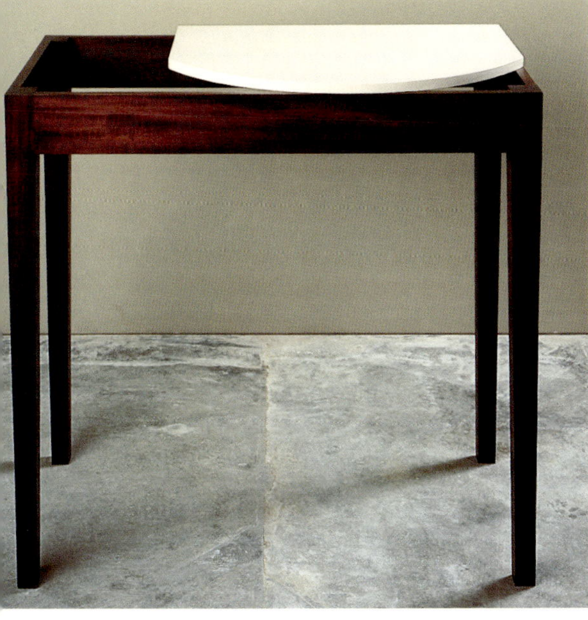

This concept of dissonant parts fully flowered in another 1985 exhibition, in which McMakin unleashed an army of tall side tables outfitted with ill-fitting geometric tops. This show at Quint Gallery in San Diego consisted of numerous identical, rectangular table structures finished with various paints and stains and topped with ambiguous yet allusive shapes. Functioning as actual surfaces on which to place objects, the tables nevertheless struggle with their implied use and appear quite unstable. The yawning voids left between the table frame and the mismatched tops make them rather awkward functional devices, and yet their beautifully finished surfaces and elegant shapes make them extremely dynamic if viewed as purely aesthetic sculptural objects. Like some sort of linguistic riddle, the works seem to beg the question: if it's built like a table and looks like a table, but doesn't exactly work like a table, can it still be a table? Likewise, the shapes that finish (or unfinish, as the case might be) the tables hover at the edge of recognizability, suggesting the silhouettes of hinges, joints, crosses, and arches but abstracted and out of context enough to slip into new significance. The openings invariably left between top and table imply a site that contains or projects meaning, and the uncovered joint between leg and stretcher symbolizes this in much of McMakin's subsequent work. As a whole, the tables are charged with a perceptual tension derived from their challenge to conventional notions of what a table could be and what a sculpture could look like. The piece that spawned the entire series is a found table retrofitted with a slick white top pierced by a square hole. *New Table* (1985) provides a "window" onto its history and structure while also asserting a new order and represents yet another staged collapse of figure and ground to stimulate active looking and thinking.

UNTITLED (SHORTENED ARCH TABLE), 1985

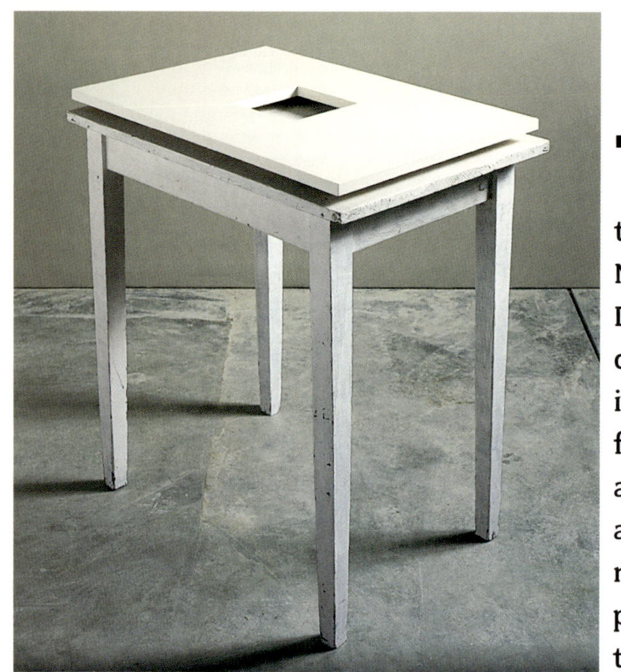

The excitement that followed this installation led to several furniture commissions, the first being a two-part credenza for MCASD Director Hugh Davies. The Hugh Davies Credenza (1986) embodies many qualities the artist would exploit extensively in later work, such as a clean, whitewashed finish (a likely nod to Gill), interplay of curves and orthogonals, structural exhibitionism, and witty deployment of decoration. The rectangular top of the credenza is partially painted white in a curving arc that recalls the shaped-top tables from the Quint show. The painted arc willfully obscures the beautiful cherry wood while also joining the two pieces visually and alluding to the Gill mantelpiece. The top does not fully cover the cabinet it rests upon, however; quizzically it falls short on either end, exposing the contents of the case. Likewise, cutouts in the face of the cabinet (reminiscent of *New Table*) provide graphic interest and show off the interior architecture in a way that does not bespeak security. The front legs have also been provocatively cut so as to intimate the turned wood of Victorian furnishings, but here the turned section is shaved off, creating planes and leaving flat, silhouetted pastiches of decoration not wholly unlike those found in the plywood furniture of Robert Venturi from the same period. It is amazing to see that almost all of McMakin's later preoccupations are at play in this work, and nearly twenty years later he is still working out issues and ideas introduced at this time.

Another commission soon thereafter, a sideboard for Los Angeles music executive Mark Trilling, reaches back to the expressively painted furniture of McMakin's dining sets but breaks new ground in terms of color and construction. In Trilling Sideboard (1986) McMakin brought together

NEW TABLE, 1985

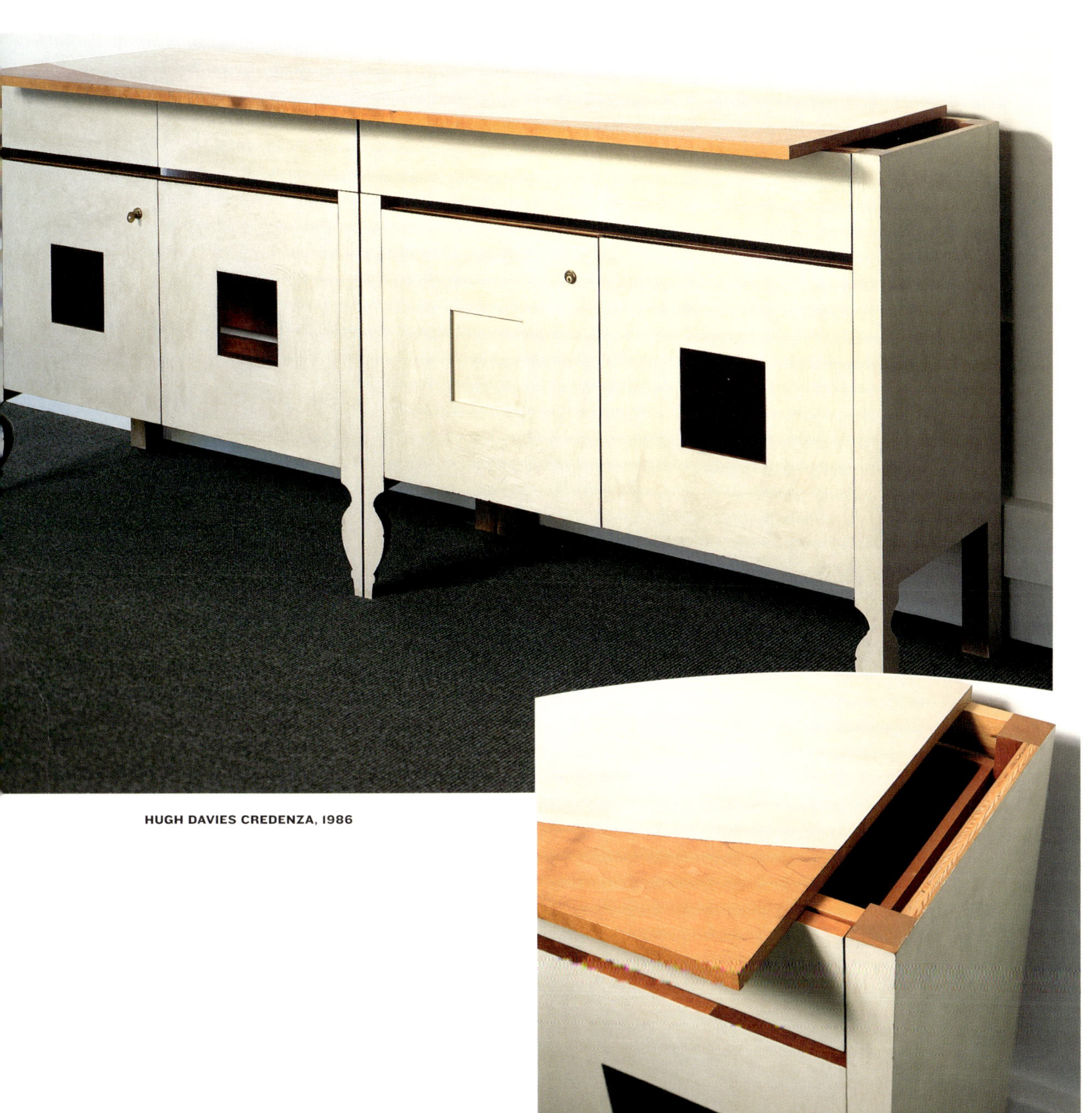

HUGH DAVIES CREDENZA, 1986

pieces of clear maple and maple plywood into a constructivist demonstration of structure and surface. Broad planes brushily painted apple green form the top and front façade of the piece, overlapping and projecting beyond one another in a dynamic fashion, while below and behind them simply joined boards hold it all together. The façade appears both heavy and light depending on one's vantage point, and its silhouette is equally polysemous, aping a monochrome painting or the headboard of a bed while also obviously up to the task of serving as a sideboard in its dining-room setting.

The shape-shifting found in the Trilling and Davies pieces was taken up wholeheartedly in a second exhibition at Quint Gallery in 1986, a further exploration of the uneasy dialogue between form and function with objects that would most likely be associated with case goods and upholstery. Boxy forms with gangly protrusions revealing orifices, hidden uses, and multiple points of reference proliferated throughout the gallery space, further confusing aesthetic and use-based intent. One tall armoire, *Untitled (Cabinet)* (1986), for instance, presents a blank façade marked only by a square cutout in its face about a third of the way down from the top. Upon opening the armoire, one notices that the top has been cut away, shelves protrude beyond the open back, and the lock used to secure the door could be easily subverted by prying hands reaching around to the rear. *Untitled (Open Display Table with Low Shelf)* (1986), with the ostensible shape and height of a chest of drawers, has a mysterious drop hole cut into its clear maple-plywood top that leads unceremoniously to an open shelf awkwardly extending past the front plane of the chest. Part Donald Judd cube, part town-hall suggestion box, the piece problematizes its assessment within the hierarchy of known objects. So too does *Untitled (Black Ottoman)* (1986), a large upholstered work that is too short to lie on, too high to sit on and have one's feet touch the ground, and yet so much more enticing and apparently comfortable than the minimalist sculpture its big black cubic form recalls. Playful and sinister at the same time, this work and a related piece, *Untitled (Green Ottoman)* (1986), thrive on the absence of the body and its imagined (uncertain) presence for their perceptual thrill.

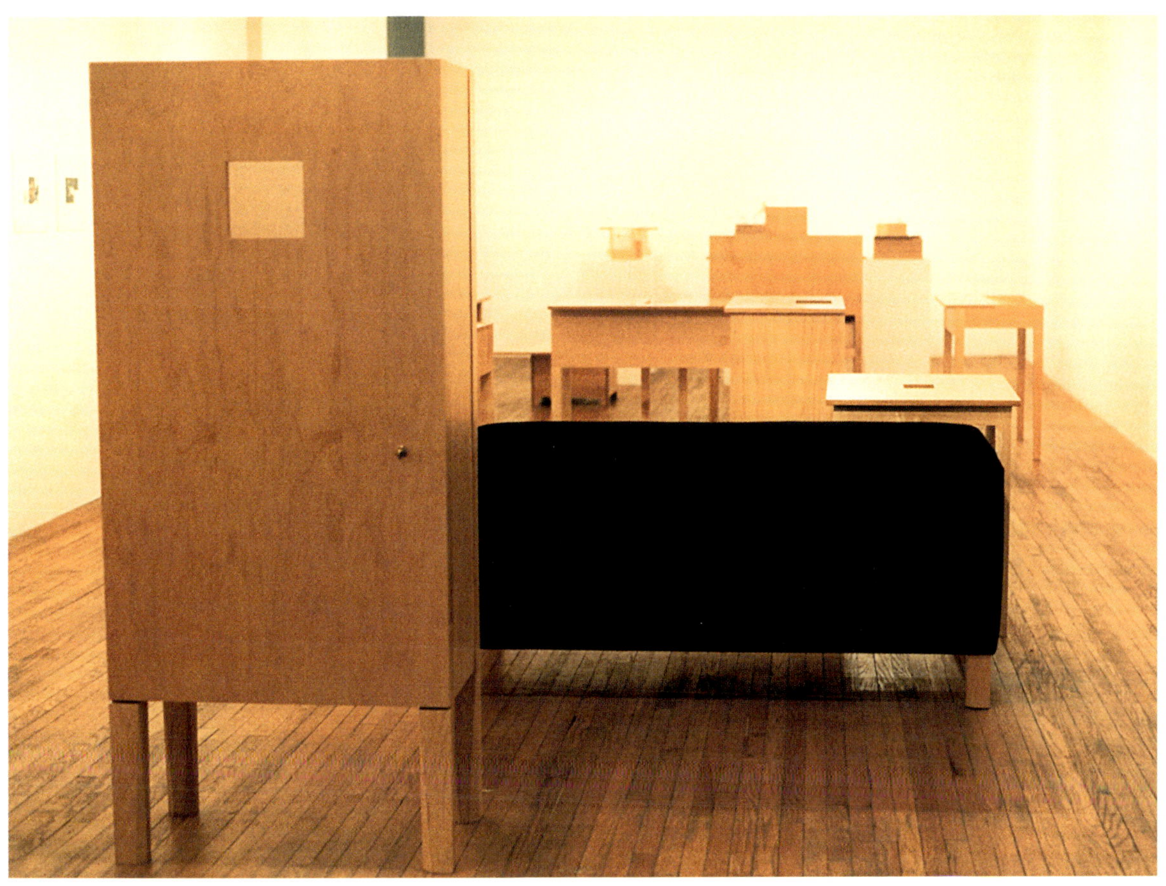

INSTALLATION VIEW, QUINT GALLERY, SAN DIEGO, 1986
foreground: **UNTITLED (CABINET)** and **UNTITLED (BLACK OTTOMAN)**

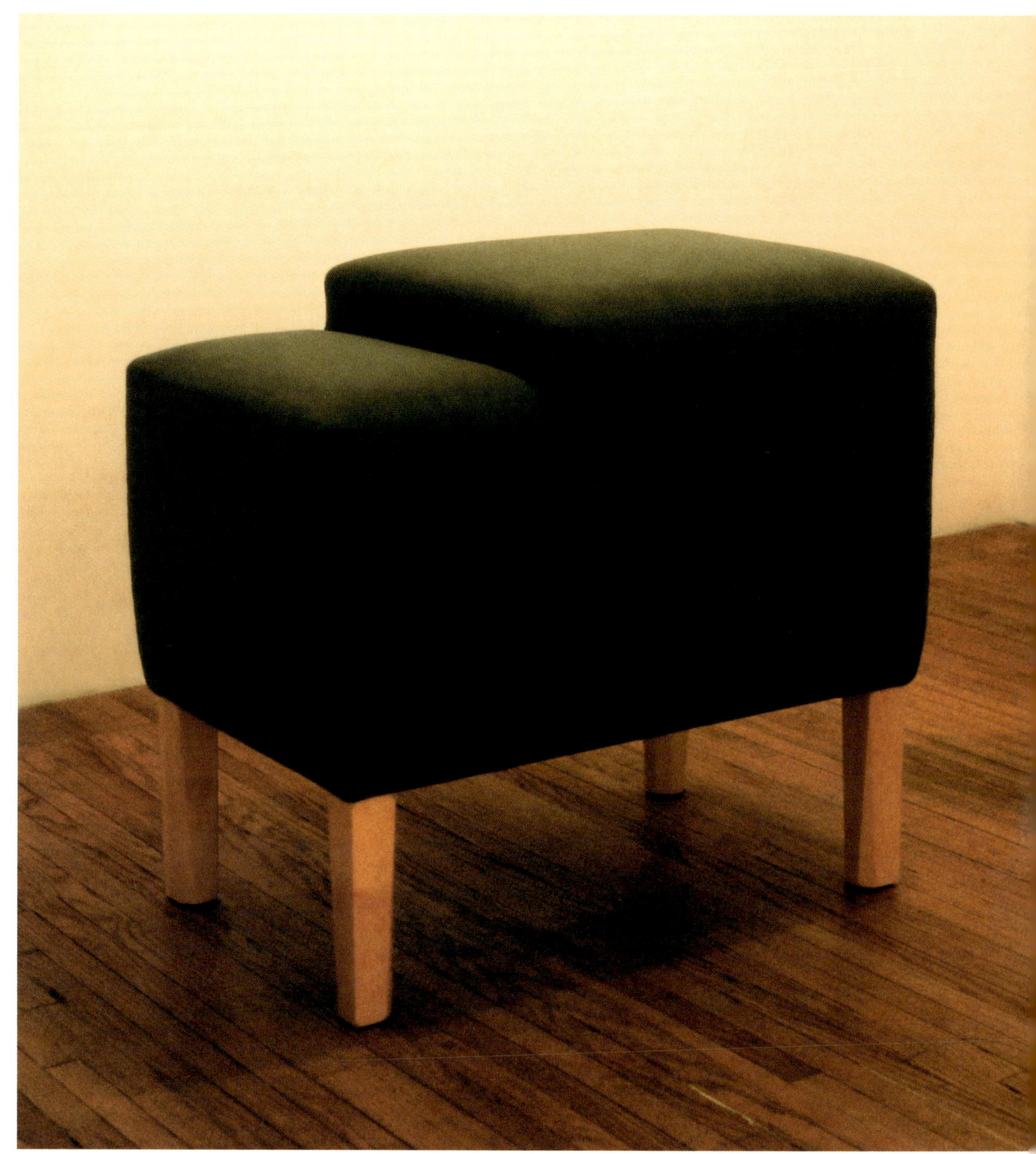

UNTITLED (GREEN OTTOMAN), 1986

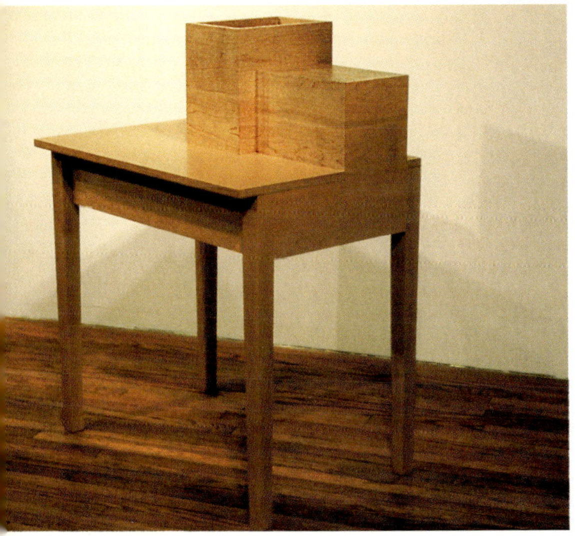

Untitled (Display Table with Boxes) **(1986) has a more immediately recognizable function** than some of McMakin's other works. Its title confirms its general composition, a table on top of which are wood boxes that could be used to call attention to other objects. Depending upon which view one takes, however, other spaces present themselves to both hide and display things, and planes slide and push in a compositionally dynamic way. One can imagine that placing items on top of or inside the designated spaces of the table would give rise to yet another figure/ground conundrum: are the objects there to show off the uses of the ingenious table, or is it subservient to the more cherished *objets* singled out for scrutiny? Another piece, *Brooke's Death* (1986), builds in a similar feature, where a dresser-like form includes a discrete display stand on its top, complete with wood backdrop. The quarter-round base of this stand is hinged so that it can flip up to expose a hiding place below, while also offering a miniature Ellsworth Kelly-like white abstraction that is as pleasant to look at as anything else one might place on top. Here too, revealing cutaways into the structure of the piece go against conventional thinking about the function of case goods, exposing an inner drawer and not protecting its contents from dust or prying eyes. The implied or imagined uses of these not fully functional objects complicate their reading, helping to push them into that charged gray zone of elusive meanings that McMakin so relishes and making them such dynamic entities. As slippery as the works are, the beautiful combination of simple materials (clear maple plywood for the most part) and Shaker-like clarity of form, mixed with intriguing structural details and evocative proportions, hinted at the commercial viability of

UNTITLED (DISPLAY TABLE WITH BOXES), 1986
maple plywood
44 x 32 x 24 inches

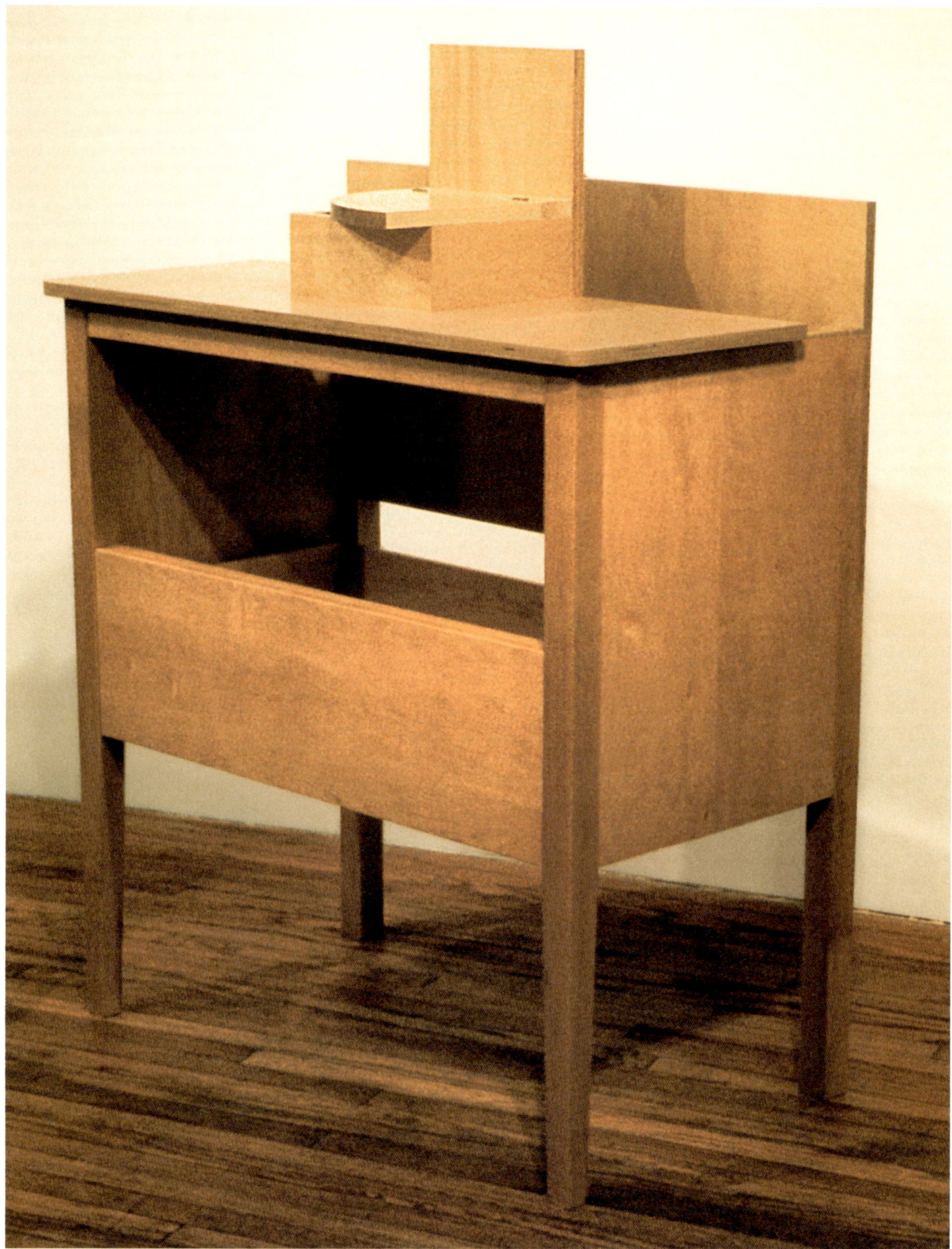

BROOKE'S DEATH, 1986

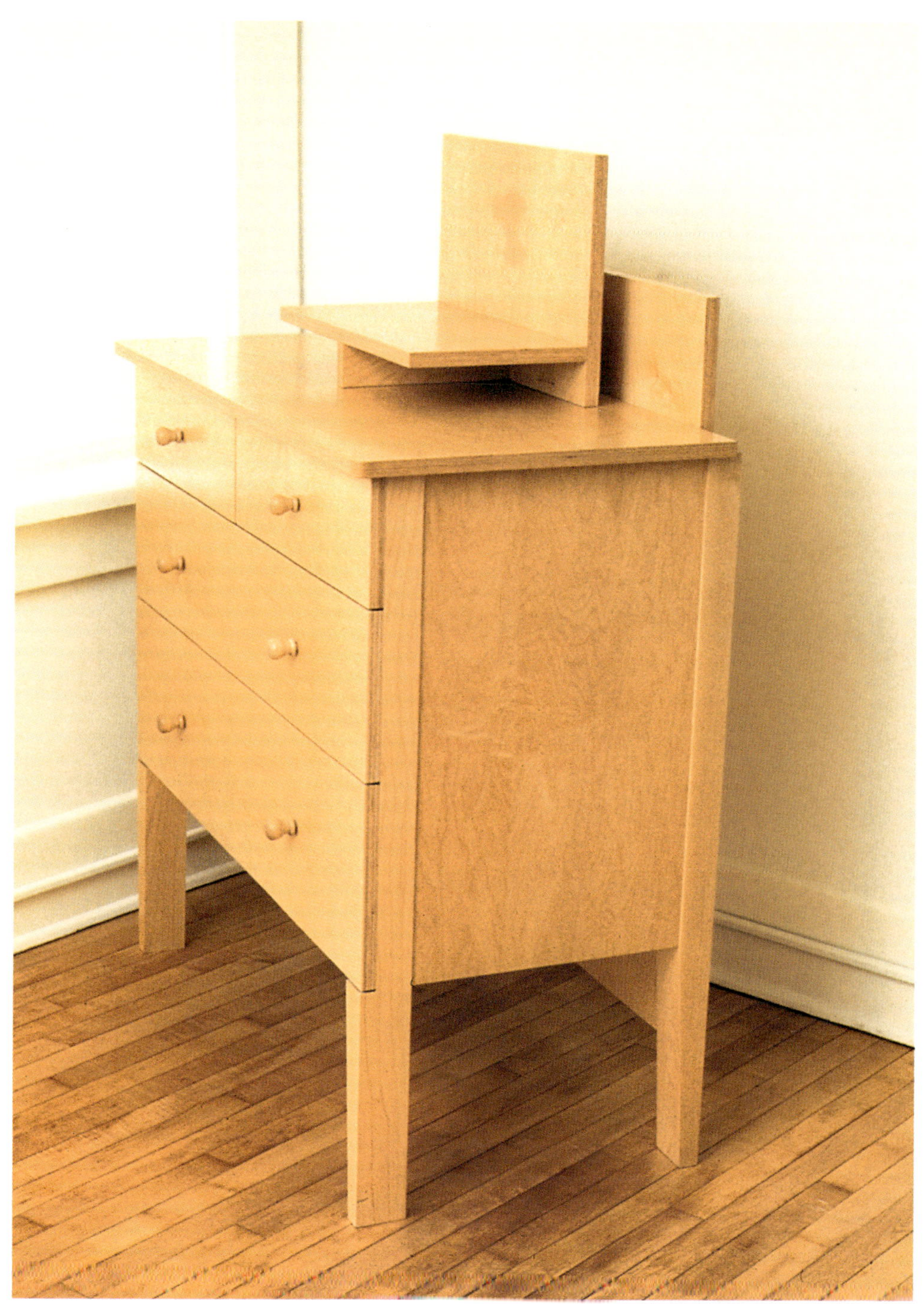

A DRESSER, 1987

making similar objects as true furniture. However, it took a drunken dare by a good friend and supporter for McMakin to take the next big step.

McMakin had for some time wanted to make real furniture, distinct from furniture-like objects that were suffused with the aura of art when shown in a gallery space. His dissatisfaction with the commercial offerings of the day spurred him to engage the domestic sphere from a new angle.[2] With encouragement and financial backing provided by Anne Nugent and her husband Robert, McMakin developed a core collection of furniture in 1986, farming out the construction of the sample pieces to various woodworkers in San Diego. In the spring of 1987, a building was leased on Beverly Boulevard in Los Angeles, and Domestic Furniture Co. officially opened. The deadpan, generic name helped to emphasize the goals of this endeavor, which were to make furniture for the home in all its warm and fuzzy glory and drop pretensions of high modern art. Modern design also became a foil for the Domestic ethos, as the kind of mass-produced, steel and leather, multipurpose furniture held up by modernism was exactly what McMakin aimed to replace with his semi-nostalgic, memory-suffused creations in wood.

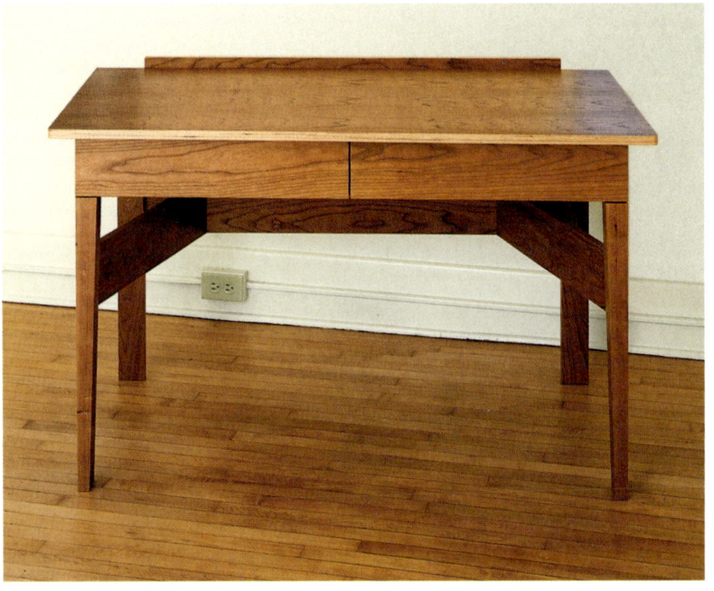

A WRITING TABLE, 1987
cherry and cherry plywood
31 x 47 x 28 inches

While McMakin had prototypes of his pieces, he couldn't find reliable fabricators that could continually stock items, so in its early years Domestic relied on custom orders. The prototypical collection consisted of a few variations on an armless side chair, alternately called the Cove Chair, Plain Chair, Simple Chair, or School Chair, depending on the detailing; a few case goods, including A Dresser, A Chest of Drawers, and A Four-Drawer Serving

Table; A Writing Table; and a variety of permutations on a simple table design called the Cove Table (all 1987). This last design was adapted for use as a four-seat dining table, coffee table, and set of end tables. All of the designs utilized clear maple plywood as well as maple lumber, though cherry wood was also available. They took advantage of many of the visual games that characterized the sculpture in the Quint exhibition, where three-dimensional appreciation revealed wonderful changes in each elevation, such as twisting legs, surprising reveals, right angles giving way to curves, and side planes of various dimensions. A Dresser, for instance, brought back the display platform found in many of the Quint pieces, offering a special spot for objects to be placed. When empty this display stand is a veritable *tabula rasa* just waiting for personalization, while also formally resembling the type of mirror often found on such a dresser, suggesting that whatever is placed there is in fact a reflection of its owner. A Chest of Drawers has a similar stage to help organize and focus attention on the objects placed there, offering the potential for an errant pair of socks to be elevated to the status of high art or decoration.

Both of these case goods, as well as others in the line, maintained a constructivist dynamism as the vertical and horizontal planes that enclosed each box were free to slide and shift in ways that emphasized the orchestration of many parts in service of a whole. This was also the case in the chairs, where an almost modernist structural didacticism focused one's attention on the composition of verticals and horizontals, solids and voids, boards and sticks. Looking at an early variation of the Simple Chair, for instance, one finds a careful, unerring placement of vertical and horizontal rectangles on the back of the chair, as finely tuned a geometric abstraction as one would expect from Judd or John McLaughlin. With its heavy back, stout seat, and relatively short legs, the Cove Chair, by contrast, bears a hint of nostalgia for the basic chairs one might have encountered in a 1940s restaurant or government building. Like the Hugh Davies Credenza, the Cove Chair and its related tables hide the curves of their legs, projecting

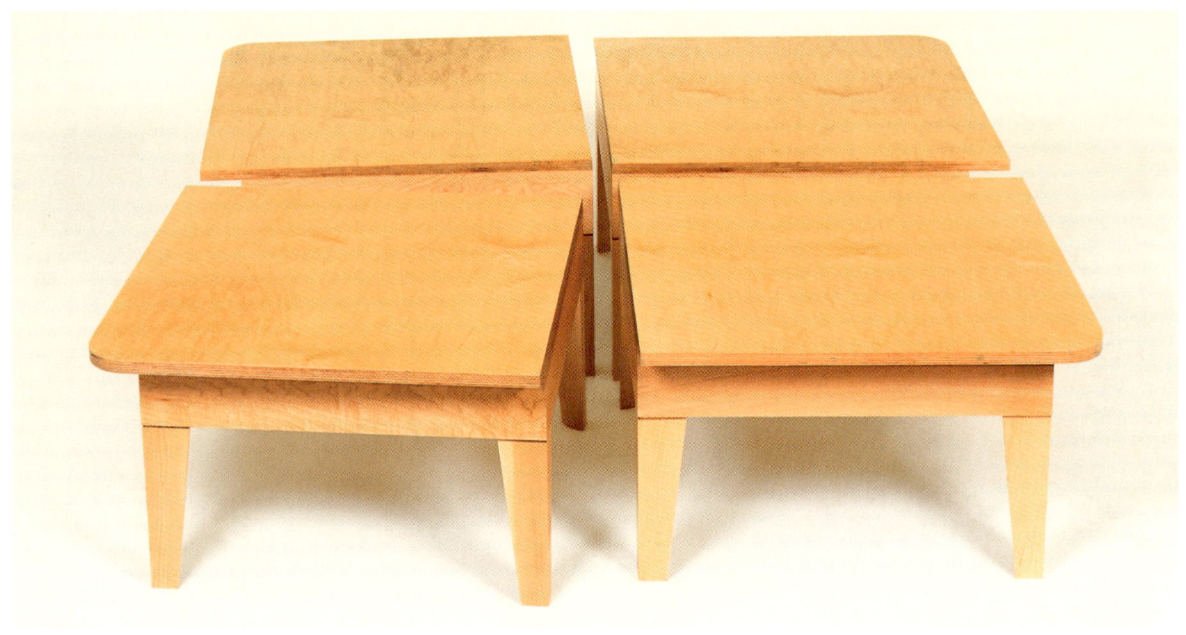

COVE TABLE SET, 1987
maple and maple plywood
14 x 47 x 47 inches overall

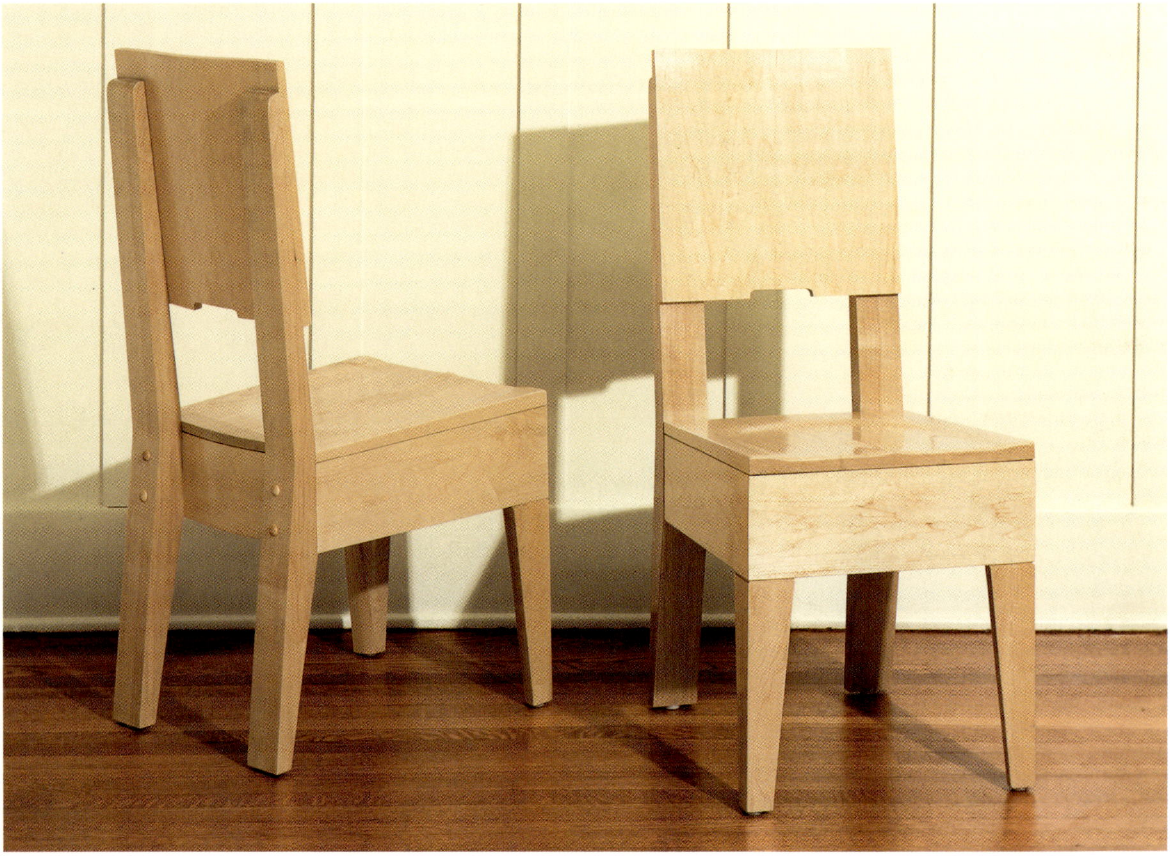

COVE CHAIRS, 1987
maple and maple plywood
35 x 18 x 15 inches each

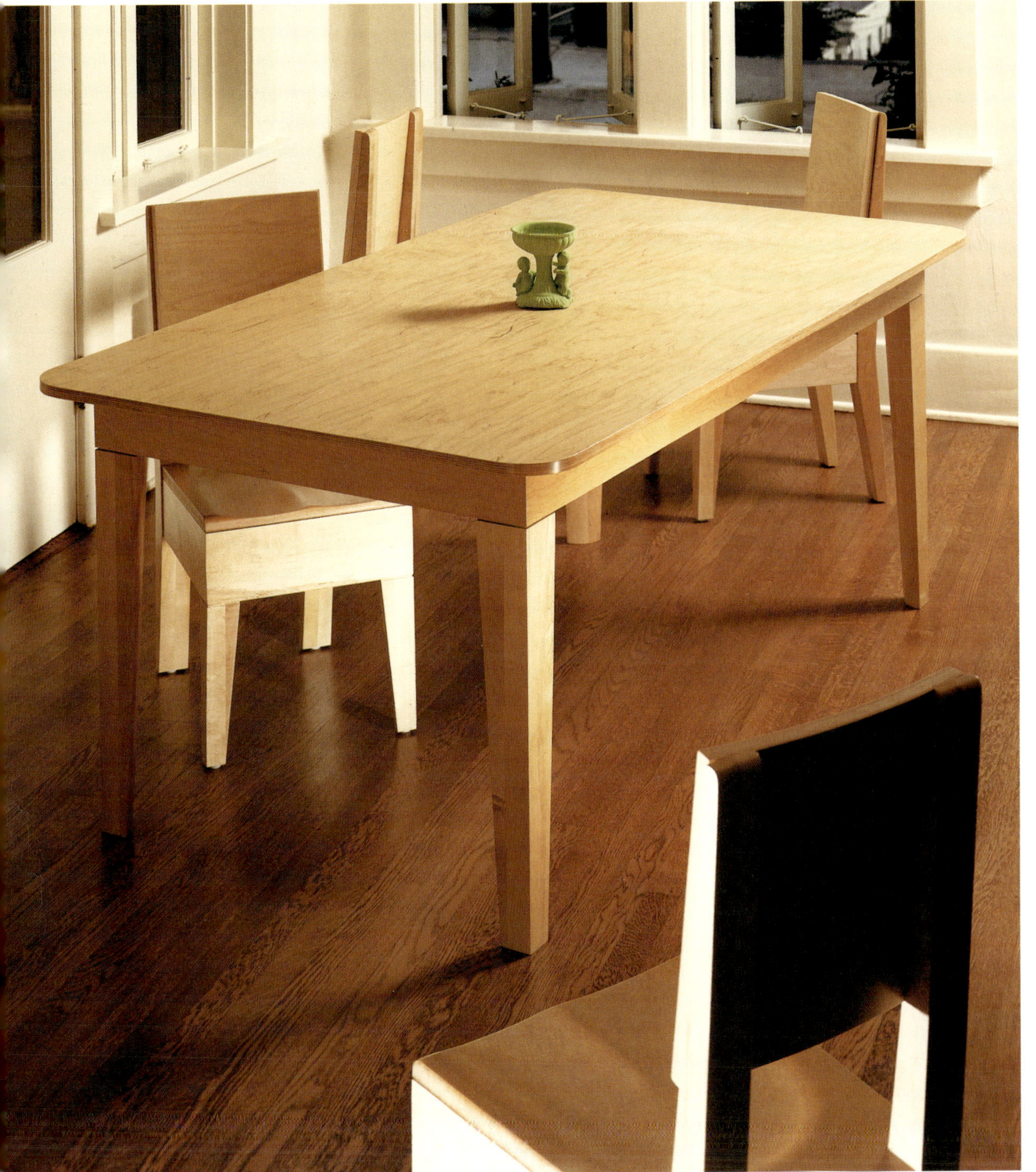

COVE DINING TABLE AND CHAIRS, 1987
maple and maple plywood
table: 29 x 39 x 72 inches; chairs: 35 x 18 x 15 inches each

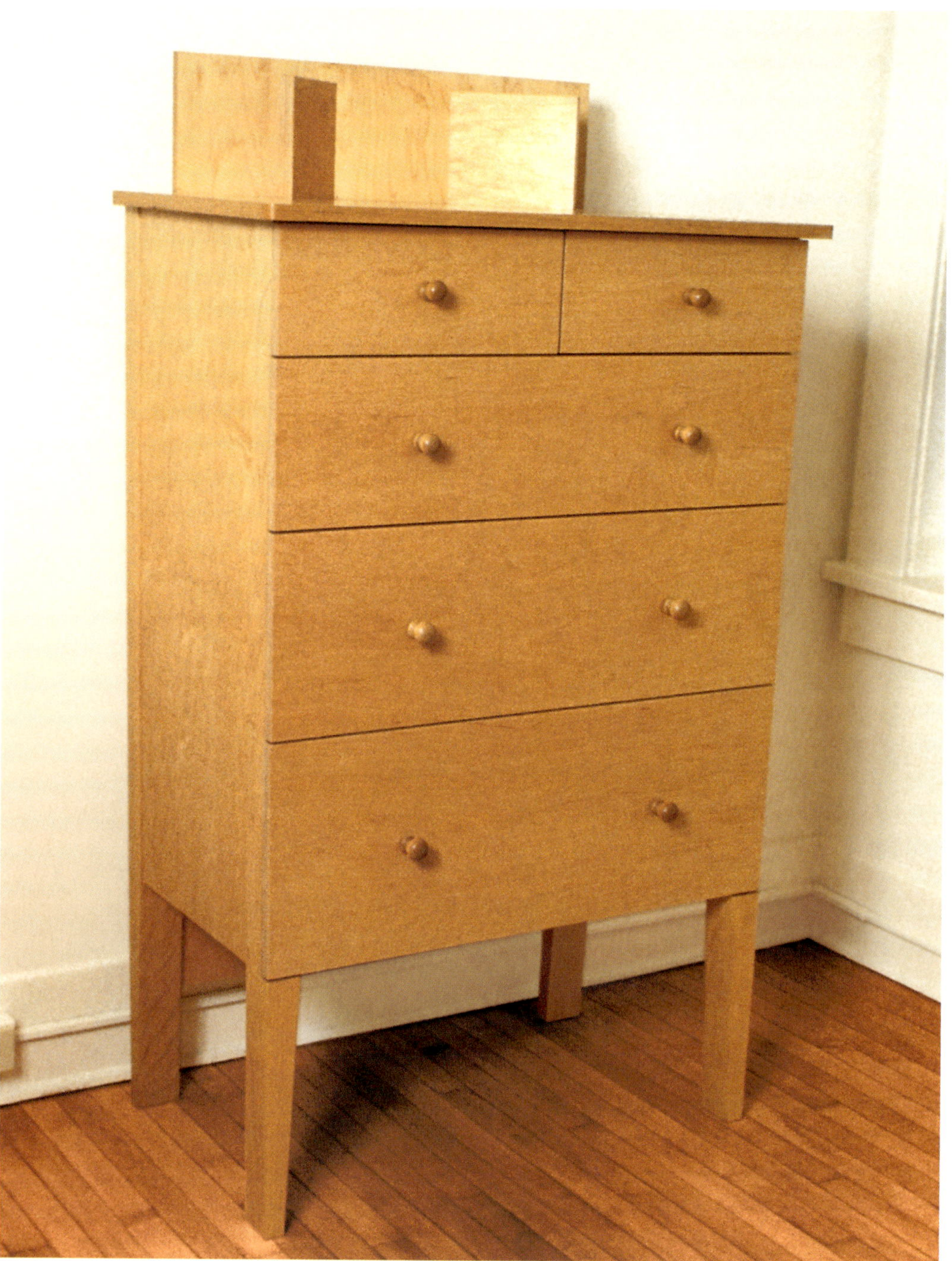

A CHEST OF DRAWERS, 1987
maple and maple plywood
58 x 32 x 19 inches

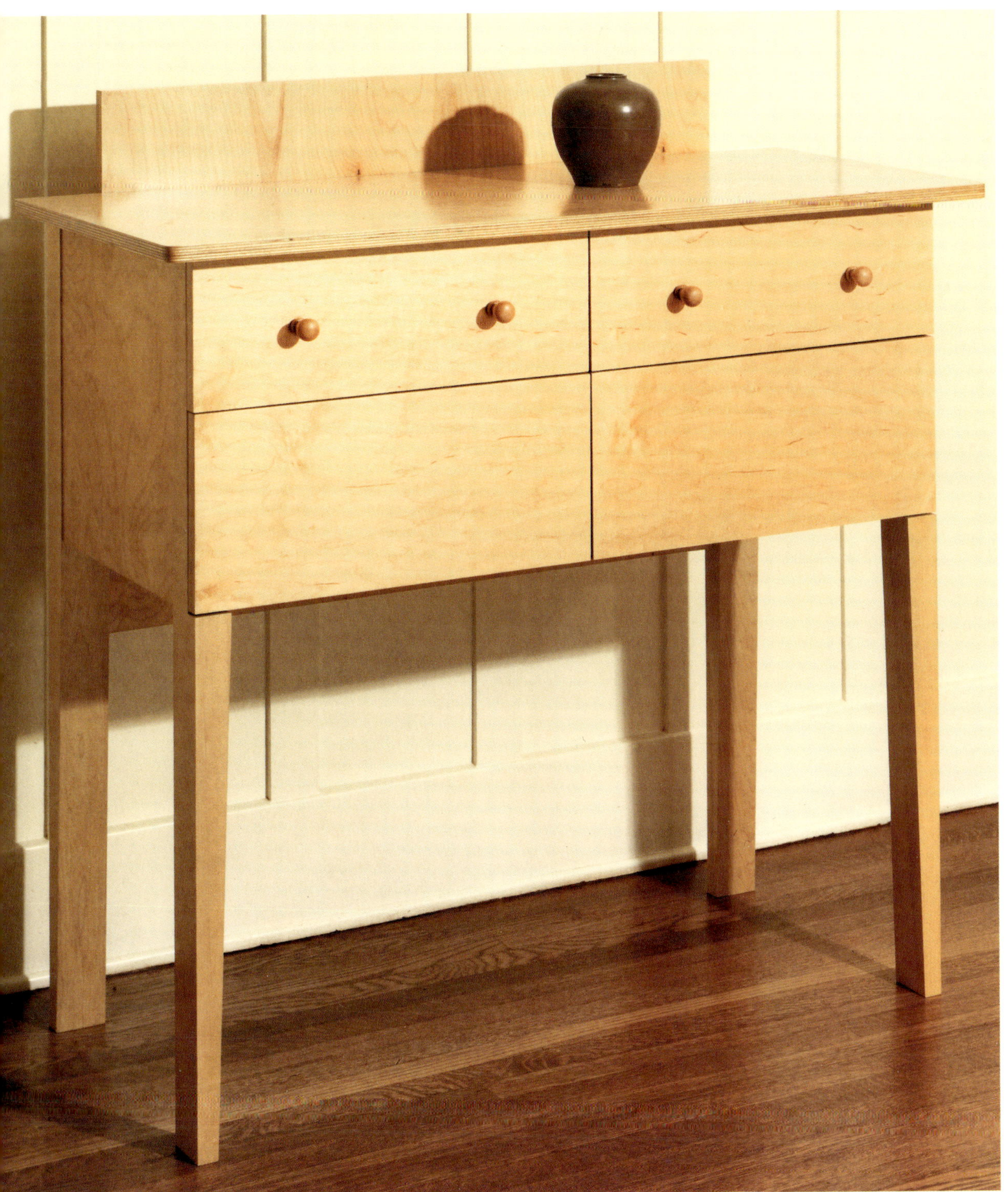

A FOUR-DRAWER SERVING TABLE, 1987
maple and maple plywood
45 x 46 x 19 inches

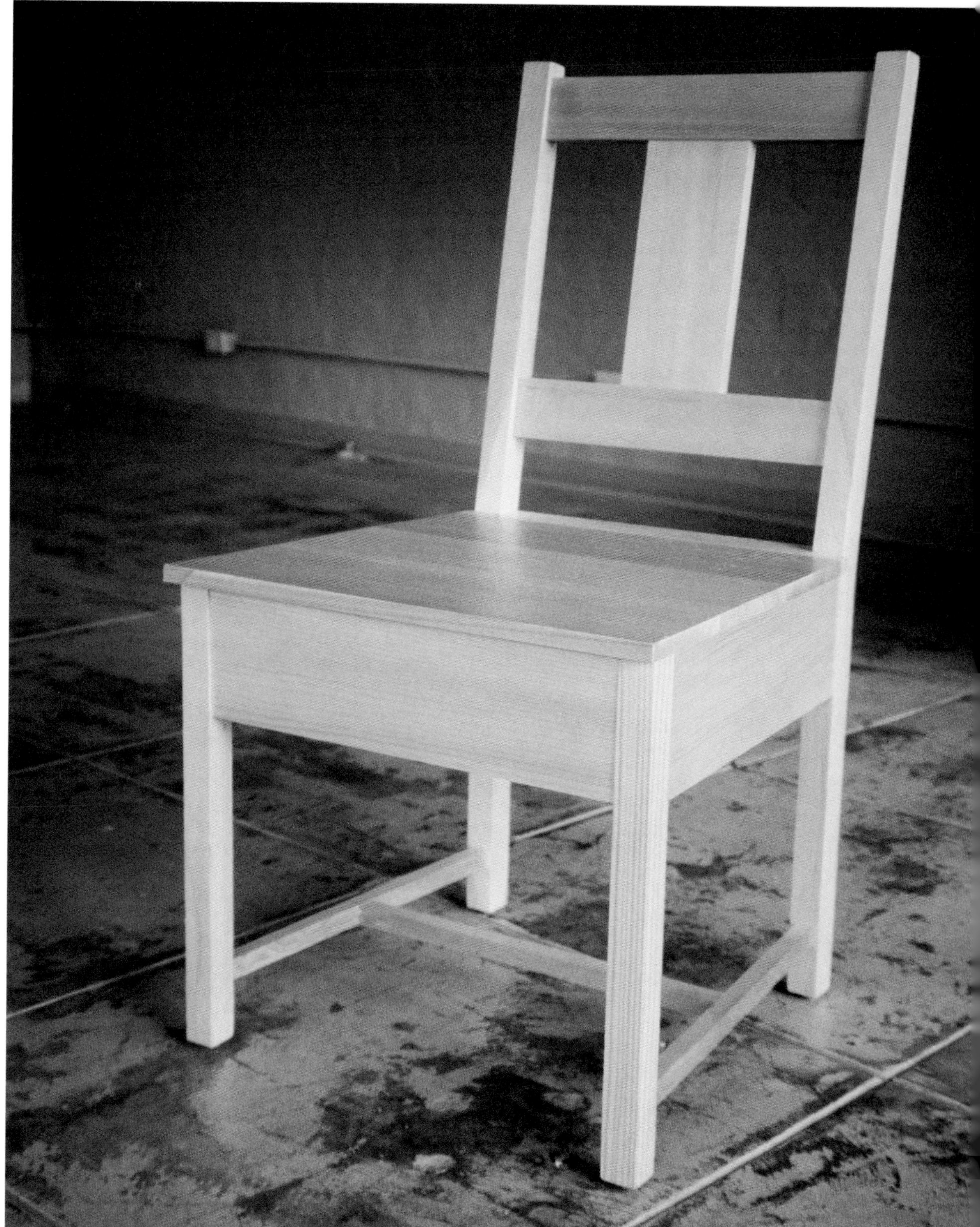

second version of **SIMPLE CHAIR, 1990**

a chaste (read "modern") flatness to the world, while sensuous expressiveness is closeted. The finely calibrated reveals between each of the constituent parts set the works off as highly aesthetic, considered objects. Yet the Cove Chair also trades on general memories of the past, something McMakin's early furniture-based artworks also did with regularity. With the Domestic line, McMakin continued to strive for a balance between visual stimulation and recognizable function, challenging composition and reassuring iconicity. How to make furniture that would remind the viewer of grandma's house yet also be relevant today was the challenge McMakin seemed to set up for himself then and is something he continues to pursue.

Two chests illustrate this risky mix of old and new, as well as the personal inspiration that often fuels his designs. Maple Chest (1990) is a seven-drawer chest in clear maple. Possessing the fine delineations and rectangular clarity of a Shaker piece, subtle details push it into a new realm. A large drawer in the upper third of the piece is devoid of knobs, featuring instead a sensuous ovoid depression in its center. This recess approximates the concavity of a solar plexus, and was placed to match the height of the artist's then-boyfriend. One accesses the drawer by a semicircular cutout in the board supporting it, which allows a hand to reach under and pull it out. A more intimate, bodily reading of this action, however, has the user reaching into the chest of a lover to open up his or her heart. This concavity, also reminiscent of scalloped cartouches or decorative cameos tacked onto less rigorous furniture designs of the past, offers a sensory delight as the hand discovers the indentation's matching protrusion on the other side, or perhaps a too-visceral shock if one thinks of smooth, round, internal organs. Cutouts on the sides of the case also give a fascinating glimpse into the inner workings (secrets?) of the cabinetry, highlighting further its sculptural, skeletal, and even architectural qualities. The front legs bear slight curves that recall the more overt designs in the Hugh Davies Credenza, winking at more conventionally decorative furnishings.

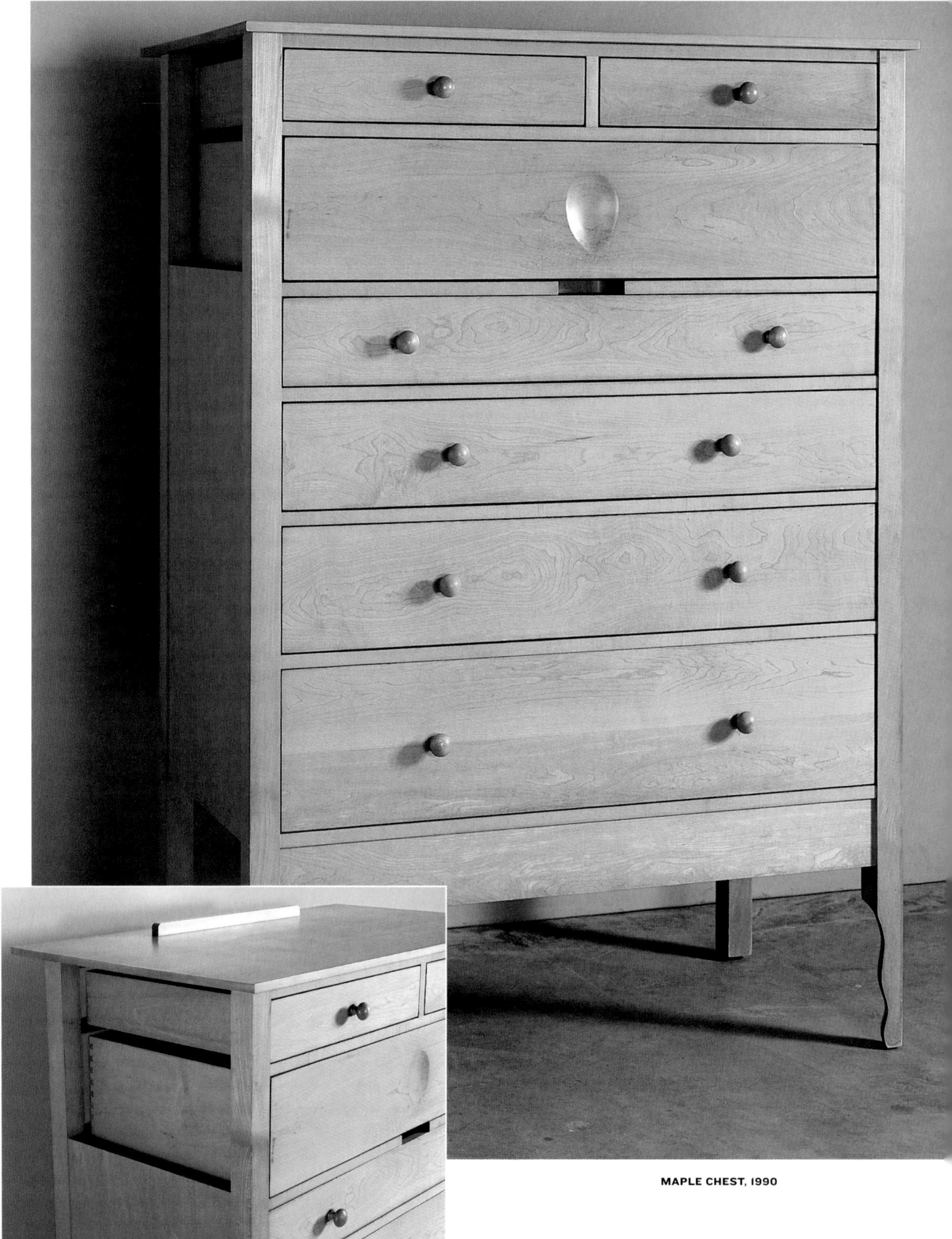

MAPLE CHEST, 1990

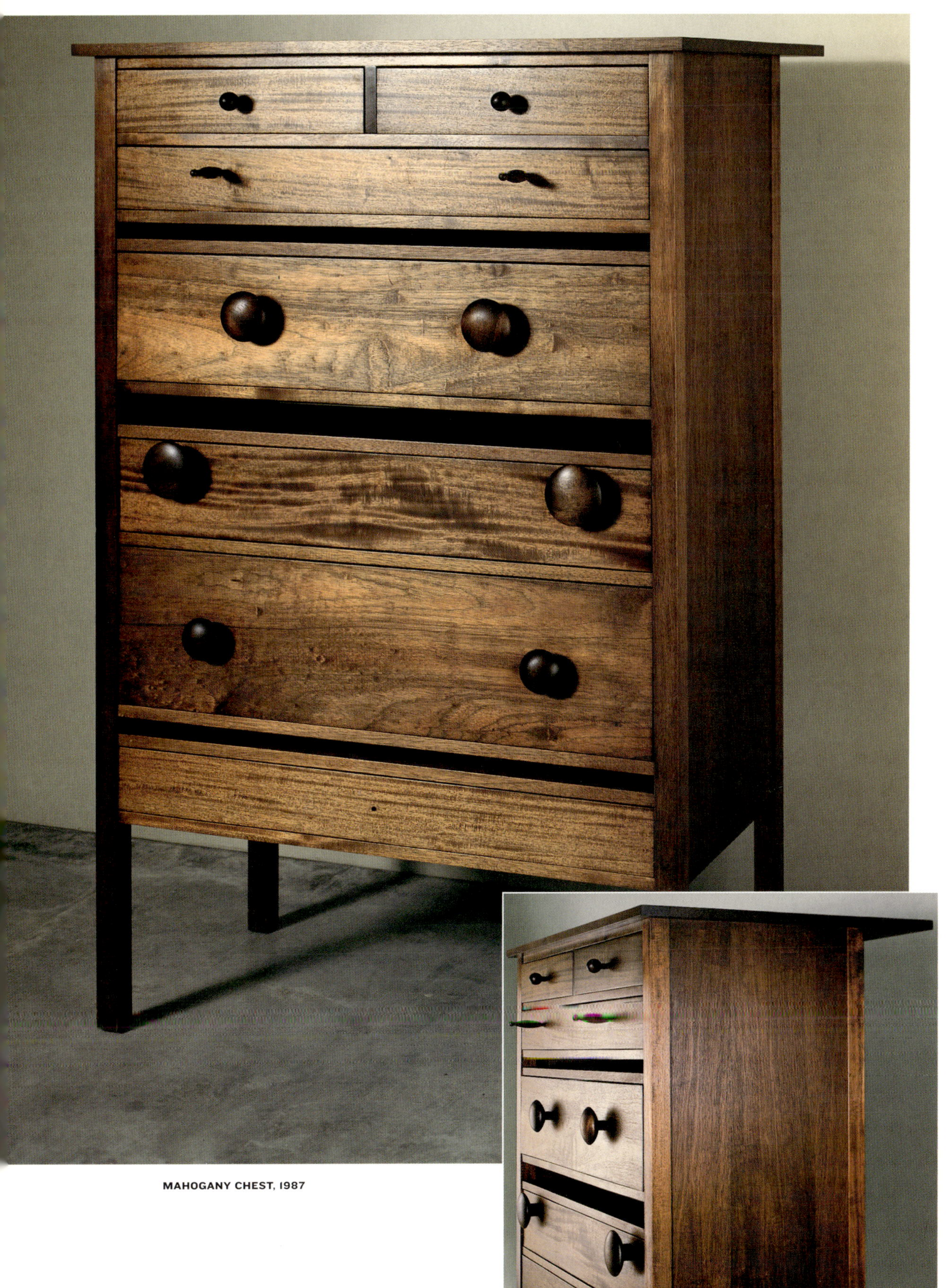

MAHOGANY CHEST, 1987

A second piece, the custom-made Mahogany Chest (1987), is built of the darker eponymous wood but has a similarly vertical orientation in its stack of seven drawers. Here, McMakin leaves horizontal gaps between select drawer courses, emphasizing again his constructivist approach, while a more whimsical play occurs in the placement and sizing of the knobs. The lowest drawer has no knobs and is accessed by pulling its lower edge, while the one above it has two conventionally proportioned knobs, centered vertically and placed a sensible distance apart. Above this, a shallower drawer features two much larger knobs, placed wider apart and off-center so that they appear to float. The next course brings its two large, bulbous knobs closer together but still centered, while the top two courses utilize two different kinds of pulls: one long, slender, and spindly; the other emphatically round and stout. This cacophony of competing knobs and enticing reveals is emphasized further by the chest's top board, which projects a surprising distance from the rear, effectively keeping it off the wall and pushing the case out into the room where light may circulate behind it. The works, enlivened with visual and referential wit, bring a room to life.

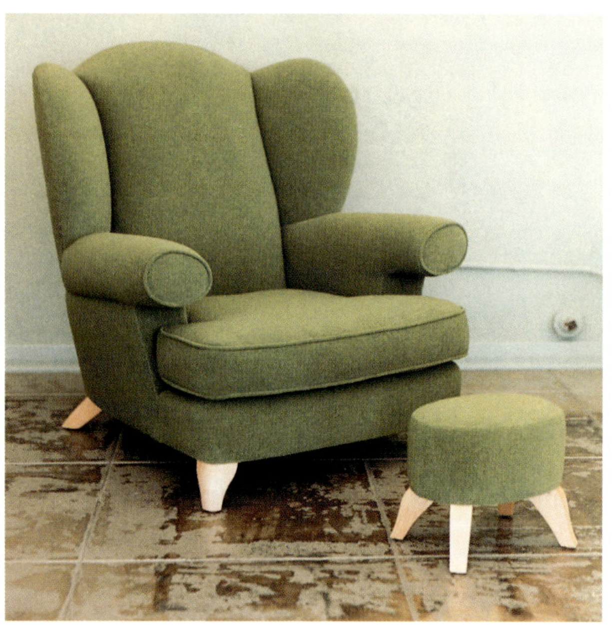

BIG CHAIR AND OTTOMAN, 1989

The Domestic line continued to grow as custom orders came in, providing the research, development impetus, and funds to expand the company's offerings. Custom pieces invariably entered the line and further diversified the range of McMakin's practice until a whole menagerie of objects filled the store. Once a workshop and a stable group of fabricators were secured, items could be more easily sold off the floor. The client base expanded.

Upholstered goods also started to appear in the Domestic showroom beginning in 1988 in the form of enormous sofas, charismatic lounge chairs, sprightly ottomans, and crossover ottoman/daybeds similar to the bulky sculpture in the 1986 Quint exhibition. At first, McMakin tended to use densely woven, tactile Pullman fabric in solid colors, either in plain weaves or subtle floral jacquards. As in the wooden furniture, the transition points between parts of the design and the location of fascinating quirks that gave the pieces their distinct individuality were areas of high concern for the designer. Proportion too was important in these pieces; they tended to be either almost cartoonishly large (as in some of the wingback chairs or sofas) or disturbingly diminutive (such as the footstools). Whimsical mismatches like the pillow placement in the First Sofa (1988) and sculpturally solid or expressively carved legs set McMakin's work apart from mass-produced upholstered furniture, evidencing a personal attention to detail.

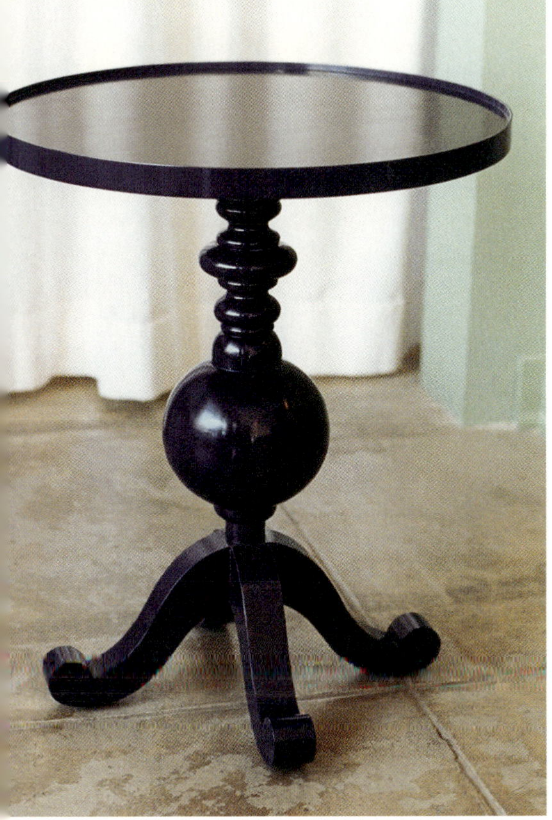

STANWYCK PEDESTAL SIDE TABLE, 1989

Custom-furniture commissions eventually led McMakin in 1988 and 1989 to transform entire interiors. Lisa Eisner, a devout Domestic supporter, brought the Benedek family into the showroom, which led to an offer that McMakin remodel their home. The Bloomberg family, meanwhile, had been frequenting Domestic and picking up individual pieces for some time when they caught wind of the expansion of the designer's practice and soon thereafter offered a kitchen for McMakin to adapt. Both clients would go on to enlist McMakin's help on residences in Santa Monica and Los Angeles, as well as in Massachusetts and Long Island, New York, over the

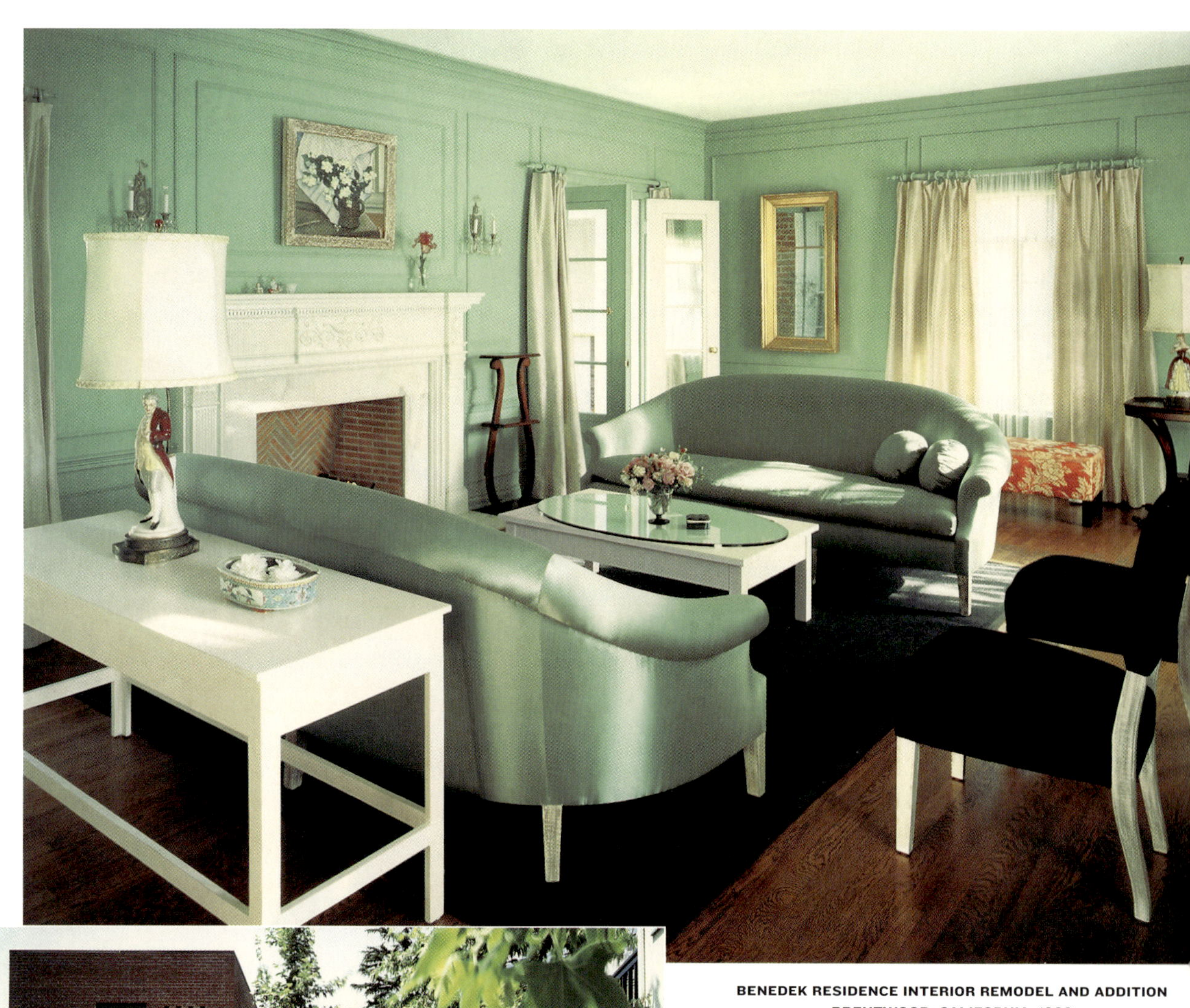

BENEDEK RESIDENCE INTERIOR REMODEL AND ADDITION
BRENTWOOD, CALIFORNIA, 1989

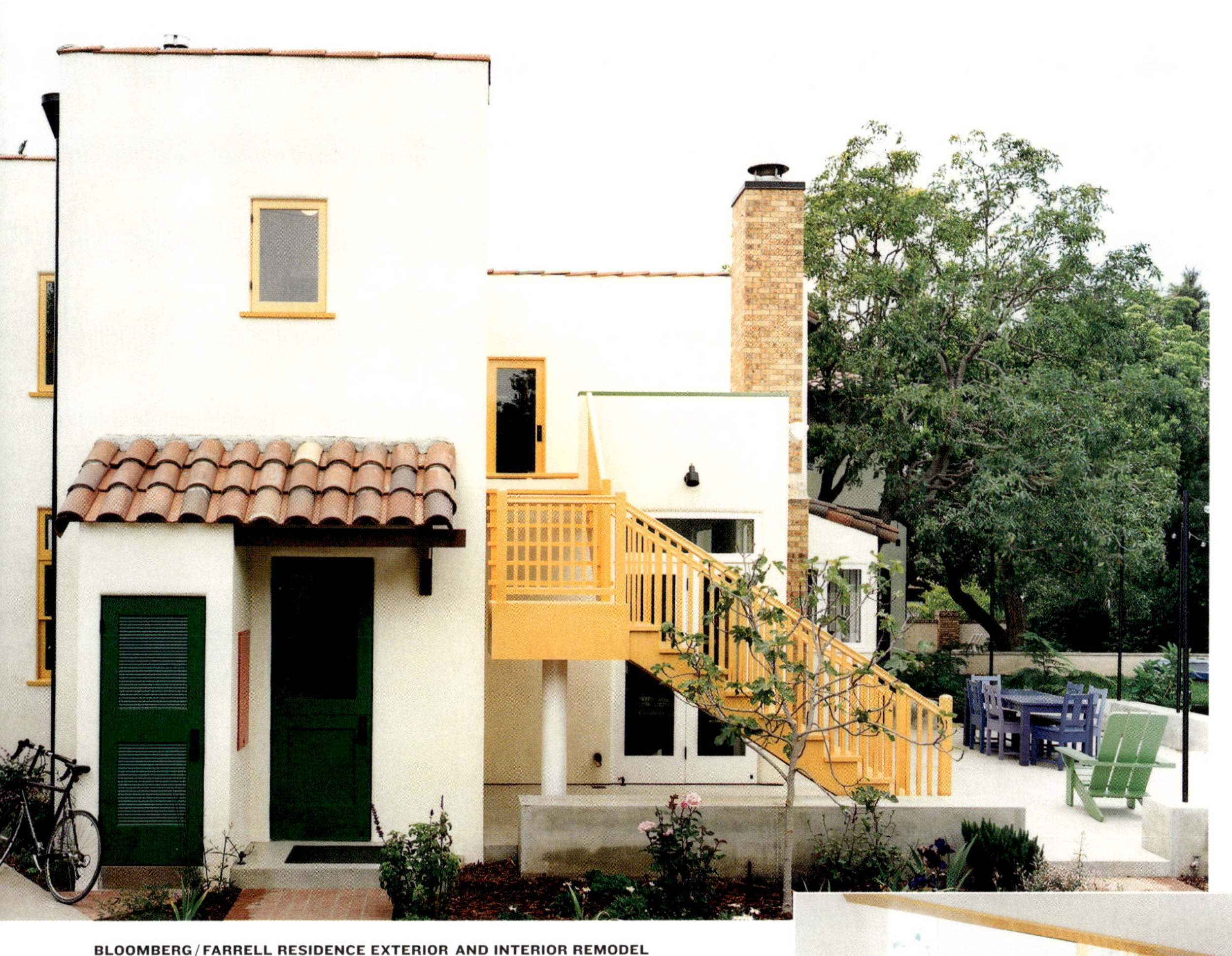

BLOOMBERG / FARRELL RESIDENCE EXTERIOR AND INTERIOR REMODEL
SANTA MONICA, CALIFORNIA, 1999

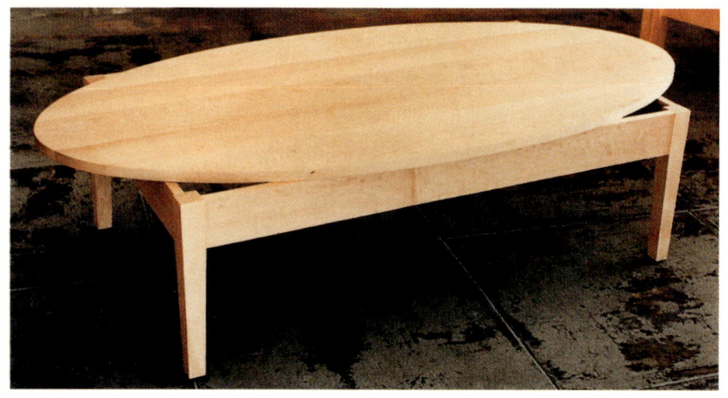

next fifteen years. As a result of these projects and others like them, more objects were introduced into the Domestic repertoire, including the Stanwyck pedestal table from the Benedek commission (an early example of painted furniture in the Domestic line and also one of his most shamelessly decorative), as well as a coffee table and side table that resurrected his interest in contrasting geometric forms through the use of an oval piece of glass set into a rectangular table. Another related piece, the Oval Coffee Table (1990), was created for Domestic out of wood and strongly reminiscent of the work in the 1985 Quint exhibition. Increasingly high-profile commissions continued to come his way, including Jay Leno's set for "The Tonight Show," and culminated in 1991 with the job of creating the image and furniture for J.Crew stores. This enormous job carried over a two-year period and eventually spelled disaster for Domestic as the sheer volume required, coupled with the uneasy marriage of McMakin's essential artist persona and the bottom-line-driven world of corporate entrepreneurship, led McMakin to close his company in 1994. The image McMakin created for J.Crew stores continues in watered-down form to this day in their clean-lined, oversized club chairs; chunky, unadorned display tables; and spare, Waspy interiors.

Before closing the first incarnation of Domestic Furniture Co., McMakin began to be concerned with the social, environmental, and economic realities of the wood industry. Although his palette of materials at Domestic had been limited to maple and cherry, with the occasional use of an exotic hardwood like mahogany, in 1989 he began to research the logging industry and immerse himself in its politics. His research took him to Costa Rica, Canada, and the Pacific Northwest; a Redwoods summer camp to study deforestation politics; and a tree-saving demonstration at Fort Bragg. One result was that other woods began to enter the vocabulary of Domestic,

OVAL COFFEE TABLE, 1990

such as black acacia in a coffee table from 1992 and fumed oak in a side table from 1993. As the materials changed, so did their inherent characteristics, bringing more highly figured grains into the language of the furniture as well as deeper colors and, perhaps most importantly, bulkier proportions. As a result of these new circumstances and his new knowledge, McMakin stopped viewing wood as a ready-made planar material for his sculptural manipulations and began to see it as a complicated resource to be understood and tracked from harvest to finished product.[3] He started to buy sustainably gathered wood and also aimed to build his furniture where its materials came from in order to foster a more mutually supportive economy surrounding his endeavors. He looked to southwest Washington as a place to set up a factory, and in 1993 he moved to Seattle with the intent of spending half his time in Los Angeles. Although he developed an ambitious business plan for diversifying and growing Domestic Furniture Co., financial pressures ultimately dissuaded him. In late 1994, he closed the Los Angeles showroom and holed up in a Craftsman house in Seattle to reassess his goals.

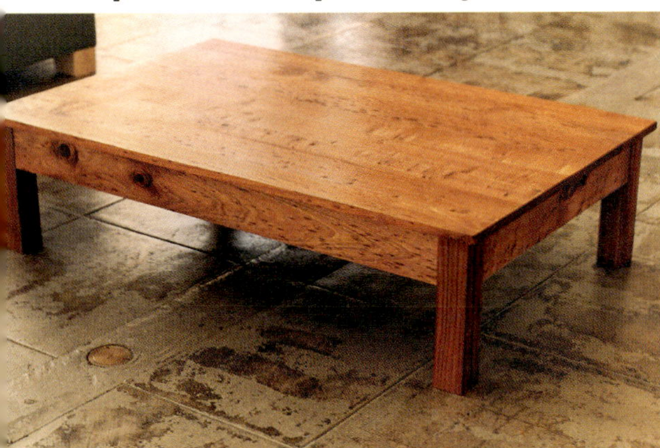

McMakin did not abandon his furniture work completely, however, and shrewdly maintained the Domestic Furniture Co. phone number. As orders continued to trickle in while he lived in Seattle, he met production demands with the help of local trades and kept overhead to an absolute minimum. Ultimately, McMakin wanted to set up a little furniture production shop and control the whole process of making furniture. When John Walsh, then director of the J. Paul Getty Museum and longtime fan of the artist, called him in 1994 to initiate discussions about designing furniture for his offices at the new Getty Center in Los Angeles, McMakin had no shop, no employees,

BLACK ACACIA COFFEE TABLE, 1992
oiled black acacia
16 x 60 x 38 inches

and no foreseeable way to take on such a commission. He did accept the invitation, however, and by 1995 he had pieced together a team that would be able to oversee the construction of what amounted to 43 tables and desks, 202 upholstered chairs and sofas, and numerous built-in pieces.

The Getty job allowed McMakin to put into practice his ideas about closing the loop of supply, labor, and product, but his idealistic approach also presented the new challenge of quality control, especially with regard to the wood that came from the trees he chose personally. Often trees are pocked with imperfections, cracks, pest damage, and discolorations that industrial manufacturers strategically eliminate. In his desire to reduce waste and embrace the natural beauty of the wood, McMakin chose to turn irregularities to his advantage. One method for dealing with these passages is to cut out the offending areas and patch them with other pieces of wood. Realizing the expressive potential of such repairs, the artist suddenly became aware of an entire range of new compositional opportunities available to him. When sanded and finished, these disjunctive areas become glaringly obvious to the eye. McMakin often played up the dissonance by running grains against one another. As the construction of large pieces of furniture with hardwoods is an additive process in which pieces are glued to one another in order to create large surfaces, the grain patterns became a natural source of visual complexity and interest. The heft of the wood also led McMakin to continue his evolution towards heavier, blockier forms and decorative treatments such as elaborate turnings. Hexagonal and octagonal chamferings also crept into his formal vocabulary. In many areas of the Getty offices dedicated to study, McMakin adopted the look of old English libraries, using chairs upholstered with rich velvet in saturated hues or colored leather sporting repetitive brads.

There was also something of the Spanish Colonial in many of the pieces created for the Getty, which couldn't have contrasted more with the rigorous white modernism of Richard Meier's architecture. As McMakin described it: "That was the commission, to bring...humanity, warmth,

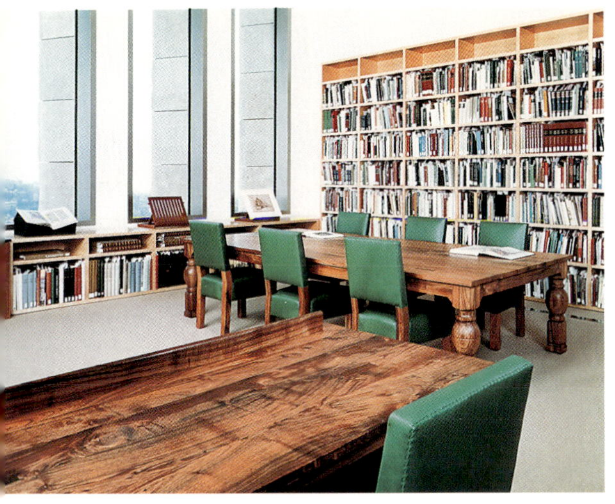

eclecticism, sweetness."[4] Meier reportedly hated McMakin's contributions, but the younger designer did not completely disregard the context in which he was working.[5] Rather, he made witty dialogue with Meier by painting the legs of his plush armchairs white, a not altogether respectful gesture that McMakin liked to view as dressing the feet of the chairs in stockings, which anthropomorphized the groupings of furniture. Commenting later on the project, McMakin said, "For me, it was taking the whiteness of all of [Meier's] interiors and applying it in a very different context — like to the feet of an orange upholstered chair. I took white and re-contextualized it and created a radically different meaning, completely opposite of what he was doing."[6]

The use of white in McMakin's work, dating back to *New Table* and some of the pieces from his 1986 Quint exhibition, certainly had roots in his admiration for the architecture of Gill. However his contact with Meier reinvigorated his interest in the symbolic and perceptual qualities of the non-color. To McMakin, modern architects often used white to neutralize and even make invisible their architecture, an act of de-historicizing that ultimately has a very historical look to it, especially when viewed from the beginning of the twenty-first century.[7] The figure/ground problem raised by the standardized white cube of the contemporary art gallery space also was of interest to McMakin and related to his early efforts at confusing the foreground and background in the domestic sphere. As Brian O'Doherty wrote about the "White Cube": "In this context a standing ashtray becomes almost a sacred object, just as the firehose in a modern museum looks not like a firehose but an esthetic conundrum. Modernism's transposition of perception from life to formal values is complete."[8] From the mid-1990s

J. PAUL GETTY MUSEUM OFFICE FURNITURE, LOS ANGELES, 1997

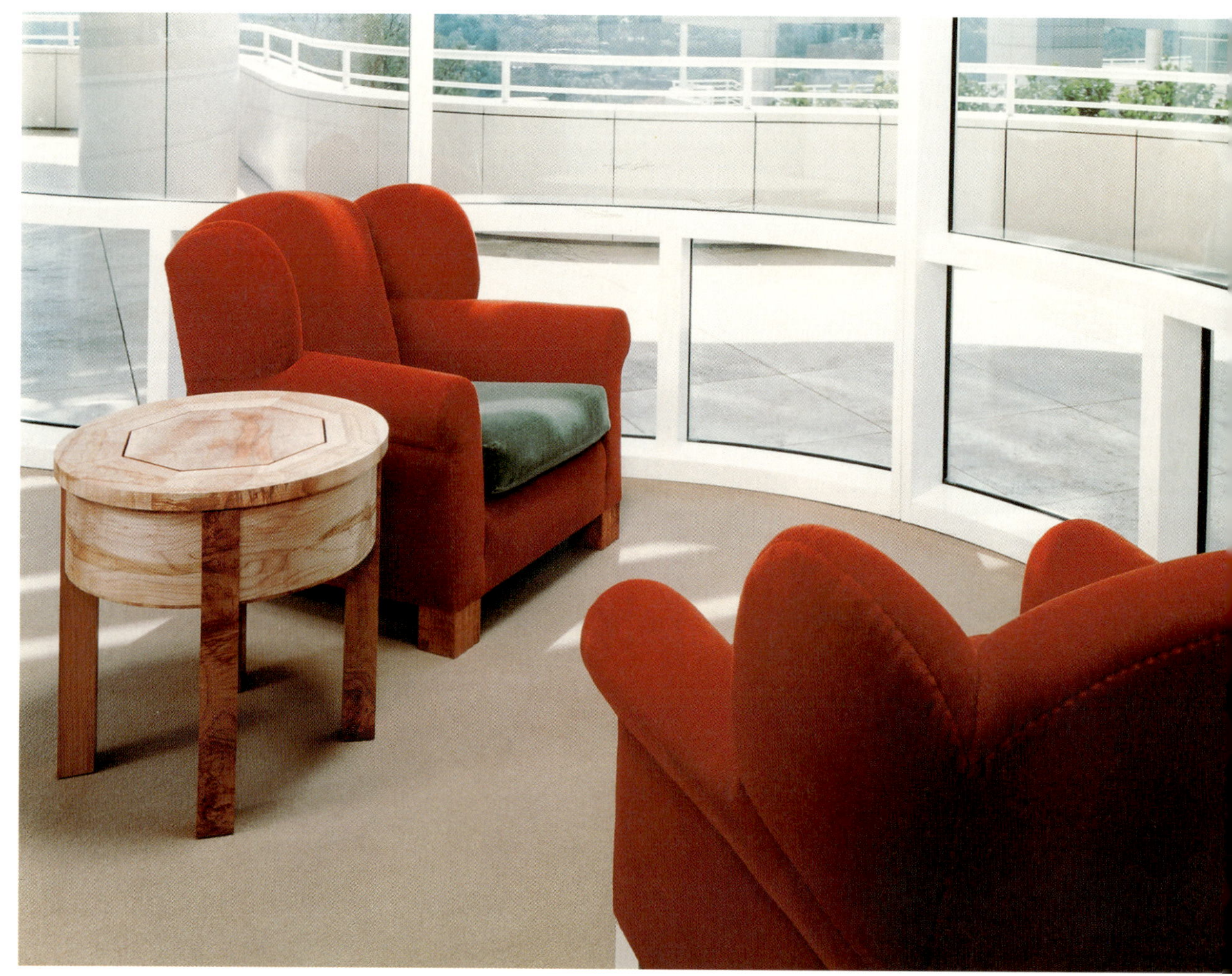

J. PAUL GETTY MUSEUM OFFICE FURNITURE, LOS ANGELES, 1997

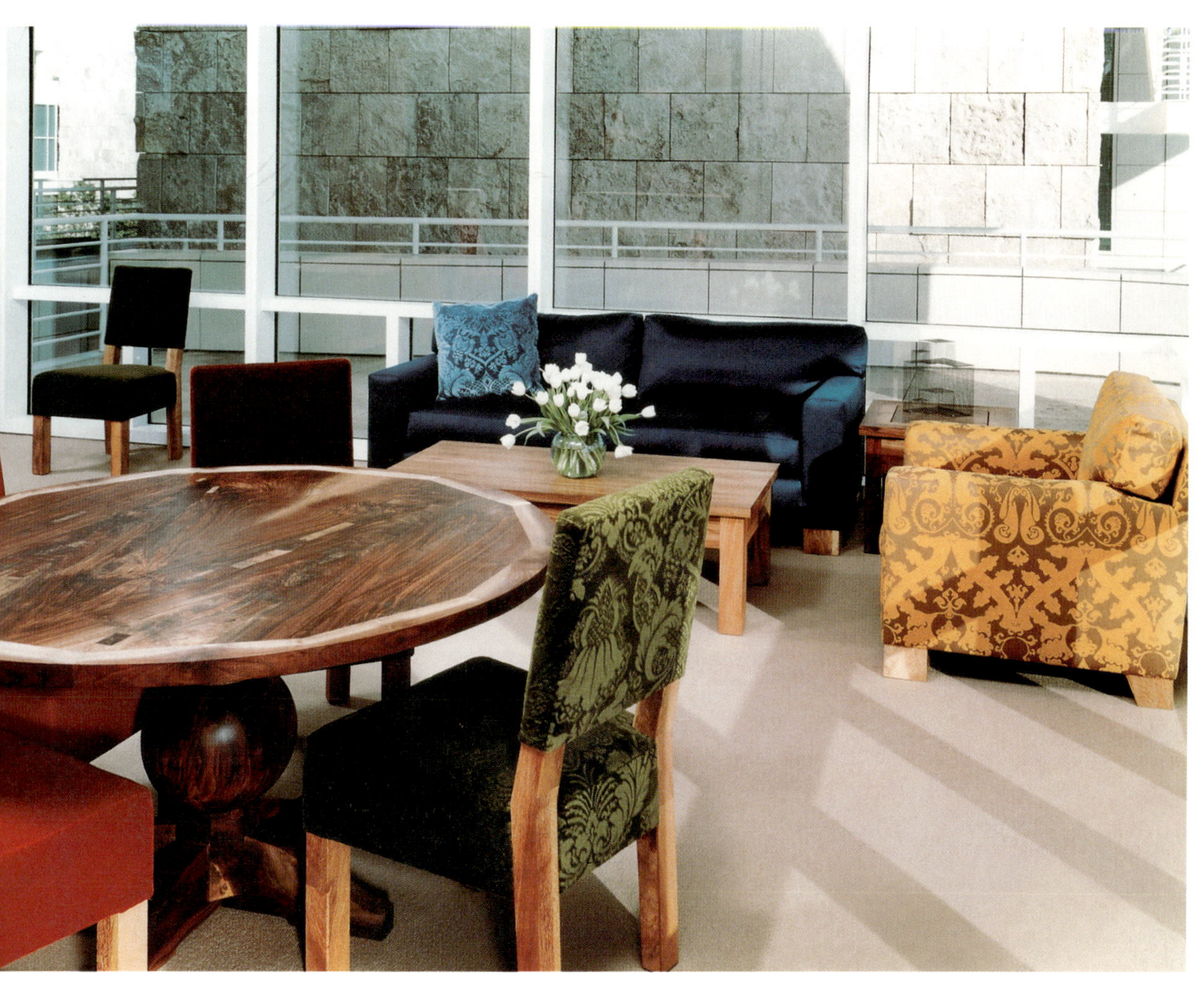

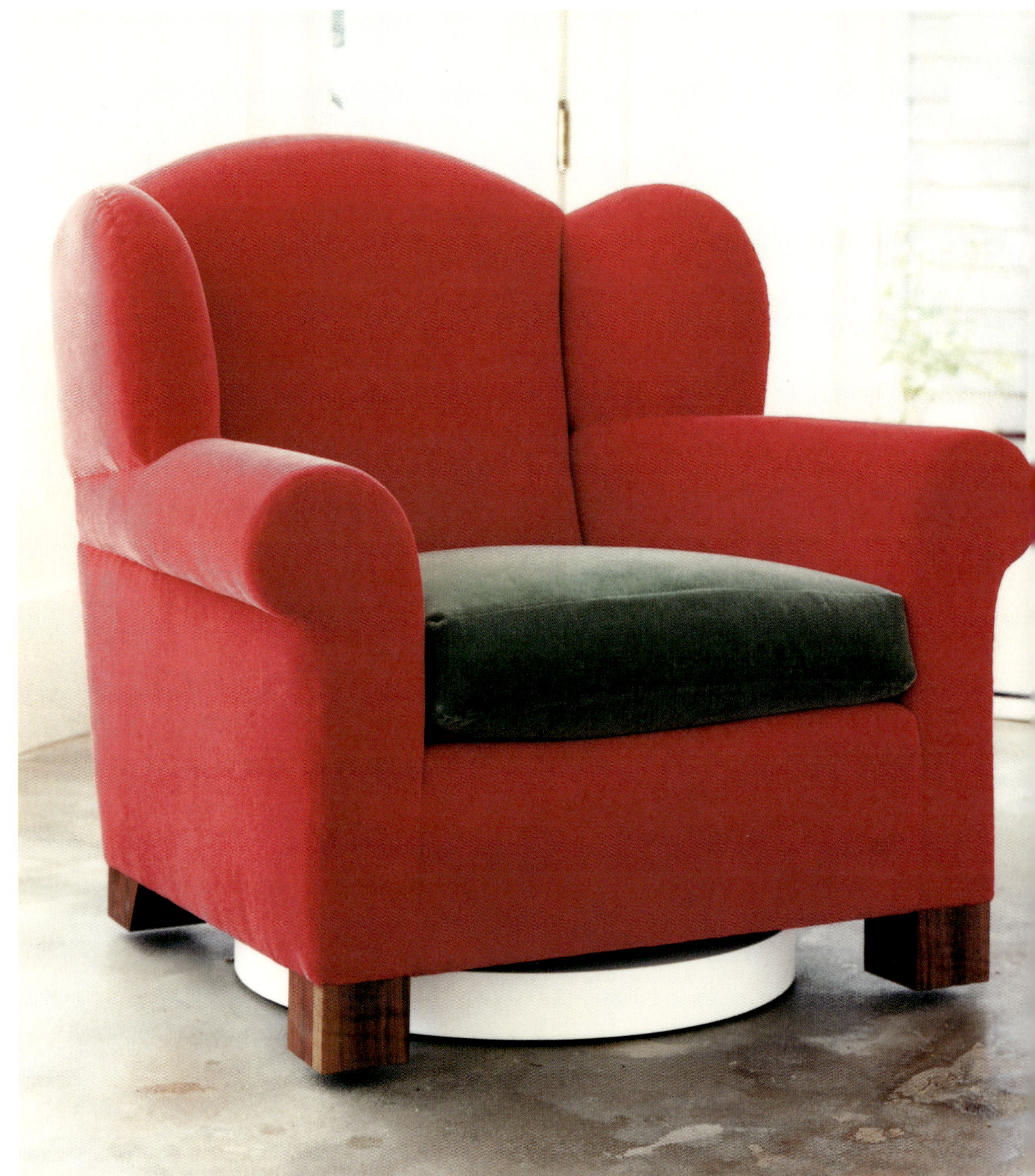

KNEW SWIVEL WINGBACK CHAIR, 1998

to the present, white painted objects have been a mainstay in McMakin's repertoire, and he often used white forms to stirring effect in later architectural works.

The Getty commission reinvigorated McMakin's practice, catapulting him to what some might consider the pinnacle of the interior-design business as the designer for a major international museum. For McMakin, however, the success of the commission was bittersweet. By the time the Getty Center opened in 1997, he had become almost exclusively known as a designer, though he had always thought of himself as an artist. Throughout the entire Domestic Furniture Co. period, few knew of his background as a fine artist, and he had not made any non-functional objects for a long time. A 1995 commission for Jim Nevins, an executive at Clinique, exposed the discrepancies between his work in furniture and his art longings, making him think about the differing receptions of objects in the home or office and the art gallery.[9] In the desk for Nevins, McMakin labored over the subtle interplay between the fine black lines that resulted from laying plastic laminate on a horizontal surface and the dark shadows created by the reveals surrounding desk drawers. To McMakin, there was a beautiful, Agnes Martin-like composition lurking in the desk, but to Nevins it was a plain, uneventful thing. Had the piece been transposed to a gallery setting, hard-looking gallery-goers would have surely appreciated such details and the piece would have been a success. In an effort to address this, he embarked on the resuscitation of his art career, not to supplant his work as a designer but to complement it, and even to cross-pollinate the two practices. The Los Angeles-based gallerist Marc Foxx, one of the few people who knew the breadth of McMakin's career, encouraged this move by offering him an exhibition.

The distinction between furniture designer and artist is an important one for McMakin, as he has consciously segregated the two vocations in practice, even when formal and conceptual ideas often joined the two in spirit. With the rise of design-like art-making in the 1990s by Jorge Pardo, Tobias

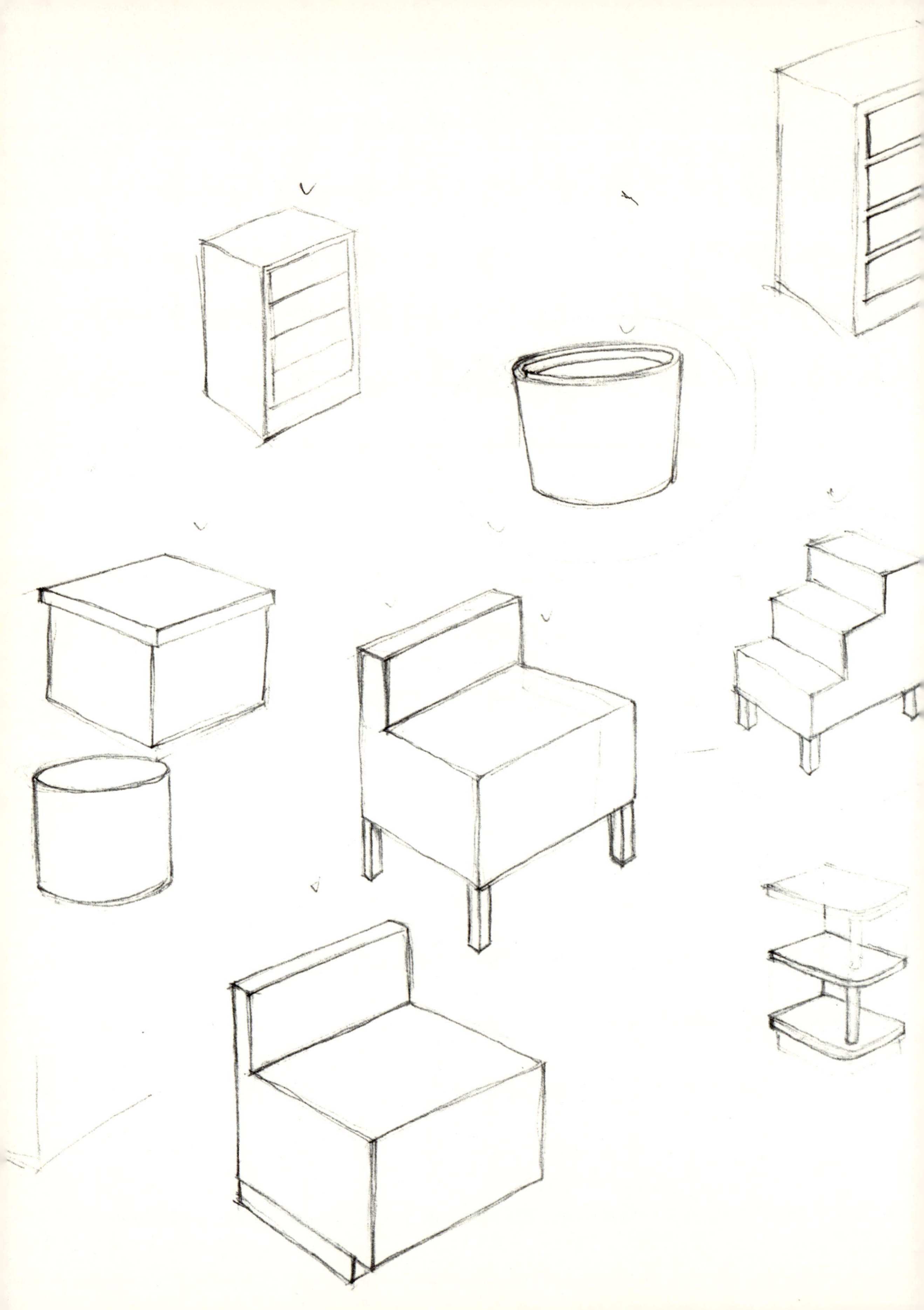

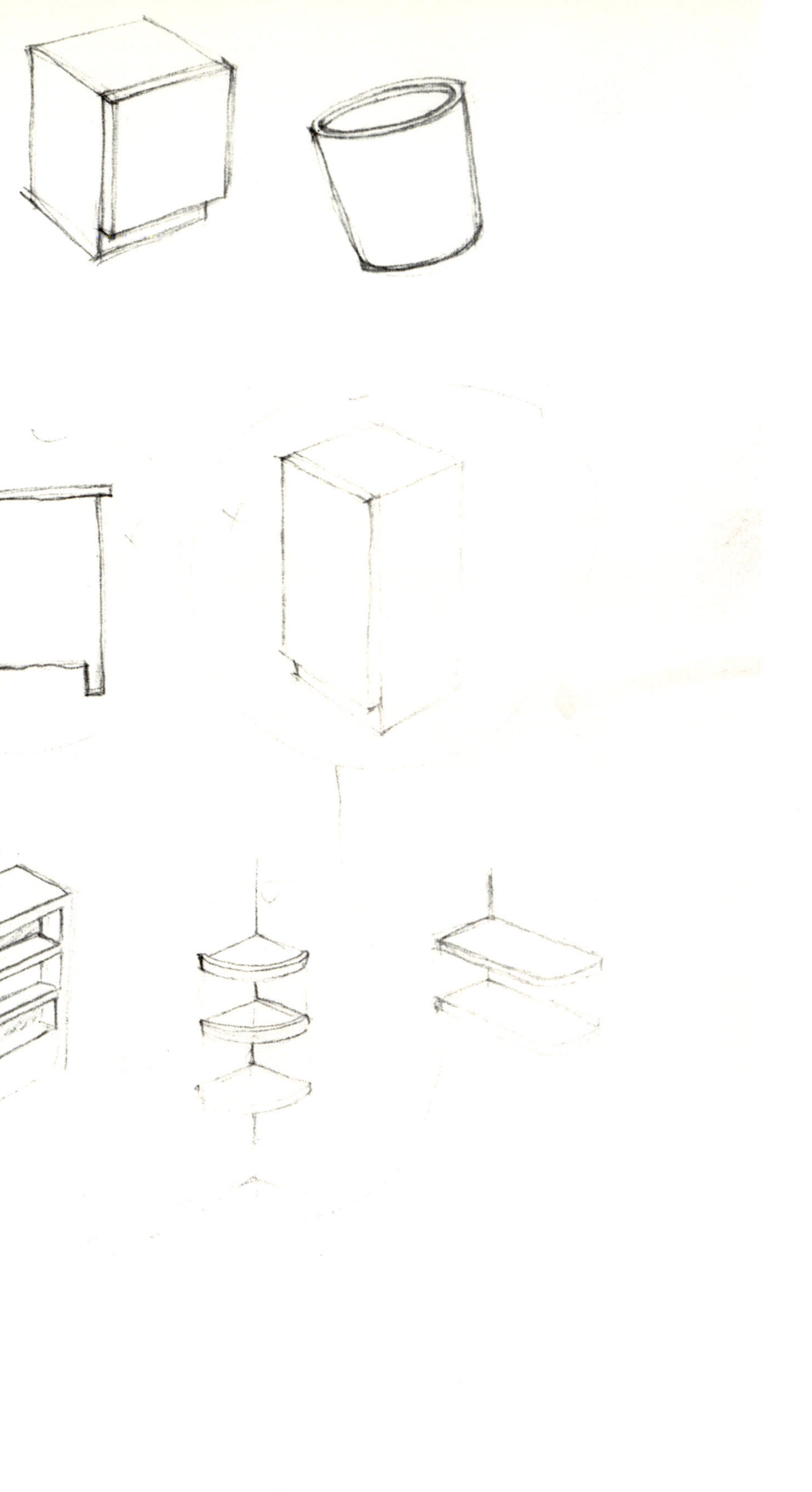

Rehberger, and others (as well as Isermann before them), it is tempting to assume that McMakin is similarly disposed to blur the boundaries of art and design. For McMakin, the differences are at once great and subtle. He intentionally created Domestic Furniture Co. to make objects that are furniture first and open to artistic appreciation second. Though his works as an artist may resemble useful objects, their inherent ambiguity — as well as the mutable interpretations they make possible — clearly mark them as art. Just as the alteration of letters in a word can force a wholesale shift in meaning, the shift from chest-like art object to fully functioning chest of drawers often hinges on the slightest of details, but crucial ones nonetheless. A door can both function and adorn, just as McMakin can operate as a furniture designer and artist, separately but equally. Even though he himself has sometimes lost sight of this distinction (as with the Nevins desk), it has emerged as a central conceit in his practice, hinted at in nearly everything he makes.

One of the first artworks he attempted as he reentered the ring as an artist was the enormous catalogue of forms *Alphabet Sketches* (1997). Displayed on a long glass table, this collection of 143 white objects map a vocabulary of evocative yet ambiguous forms drawn from the realms of architecture, urbanism, and domesticity. Painted with a smooth, uninflected coat of white paint, the objects suggest buildings, hearths, windows, swing sets, paper-towel holders, and cups but never become them, creating a metropolis of multivalent forms leveled by uniform scale and color. The overwhelming whiteness plays with his distrust of modernist neutrality and abstraction, since even hygienically whitewashed objects (or buildings) embody strongly evocative qualities as they strive to shed trappings of the past. The powerful rush of associations emanating from McMakin's white encyclopedia of forms illustrates architectural historian Mark Wigley's comment that "clearly the white wall is far from neutral or silent. For the modern architect, it speaks volumes. Indeed, nothing is louder. The white wall is precisely not blank."[10]

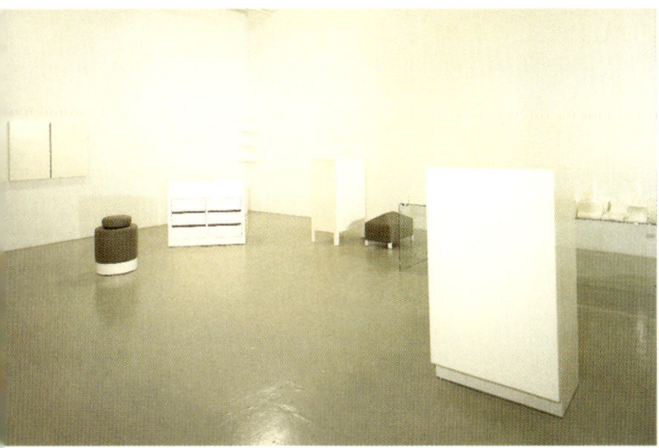

Almost concurrently with the opening of the Getty Center, *Alphabet Sketches* debuted at Marc Foxx in Santa Monica as McMakin's first gallery exhibition in ten years. Shown alongside it were numerous other larger-scaled sculptural objects from 1997 that played on familiar associations and referents but almost surreally denied their apparent function. *Untitled (Upholstered Ottoman)* for instance marries a gabled-roof form with a cozy sitting device, disallowing either reading to lodge itself comfortably in the viewer's mind, while *Untitled (Upholstered Chair)* toyed with the danger inherent in bringing a fireplace hearth in contact with a cushioned seat. *Untitled (Upholstered Stool)* likewise thwarts and invites use in equal measure, its tippy tuft foretelling a fall from grace. This exhibition also included many white painted-wood forms that have become a staple of McMakin's art practice in their conflation of domestic and minimalist forms. *Untitled (Four-Shelf Case with Reveal)* is one such object: it appears to be a standard white refrigerator from one angle and a generous bookshelf from another. *Untitled (Five-Drawer Chest)* shows McMakin at his most subtle and confounding. A functioning chest of drawers so reductive and pristine that, with its exacting gaps between drawers and casework, cannot help but be viewed as a minimal geometric sculpture, it finally put the Nevins desk conundrum to rest (and to the test).

The Getty commission and Marc Foxx exhibition ushered in a period of extreme productivity and creativity that has continued unabated to this day. Domestic Furniture Co. has risen again with reintroductions of classic Domestic pieces such as the Simple Chair in 1999, now offered in patchy wood, brightly painted, and variously scaled versions; or the Would Modern Chair (1999), a new adaptation of the original Cove Chair. Favorite touchstones

INSTALLATION VIEW
MARC FOXX, SANTA MONICA, CALIFORNIA, 1997

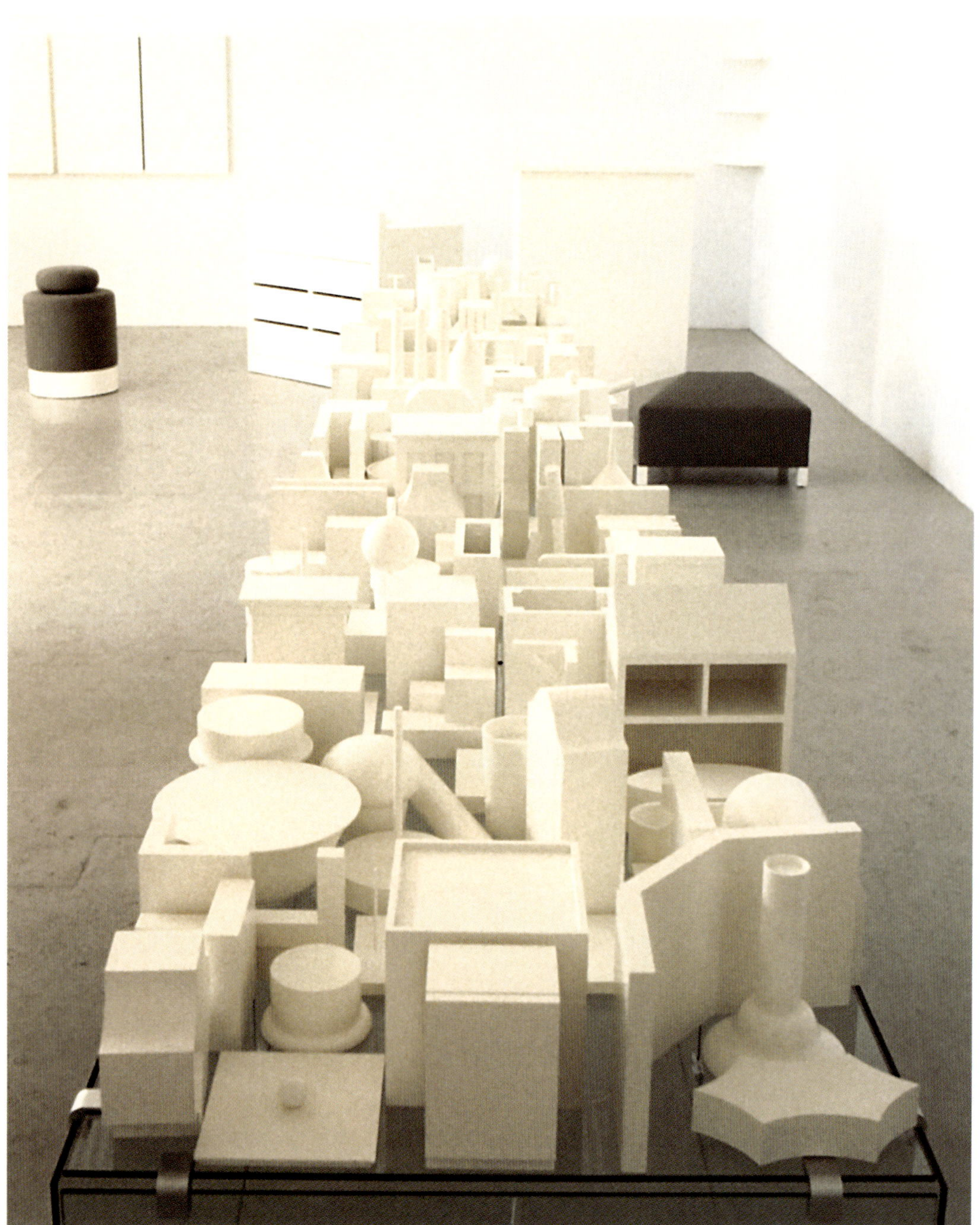

ALPHABET SKETCHES, 1997

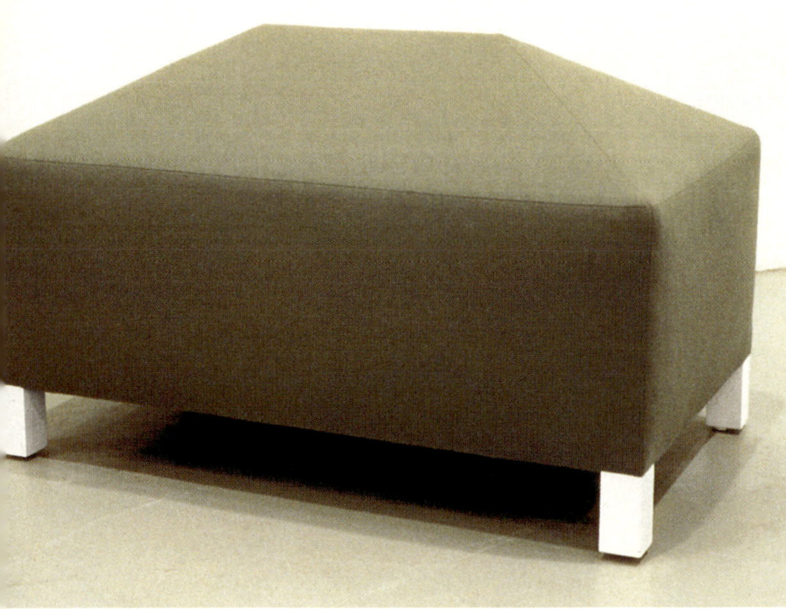

UNTITLED (UPHOLSTERED OTTOMAN), 1997

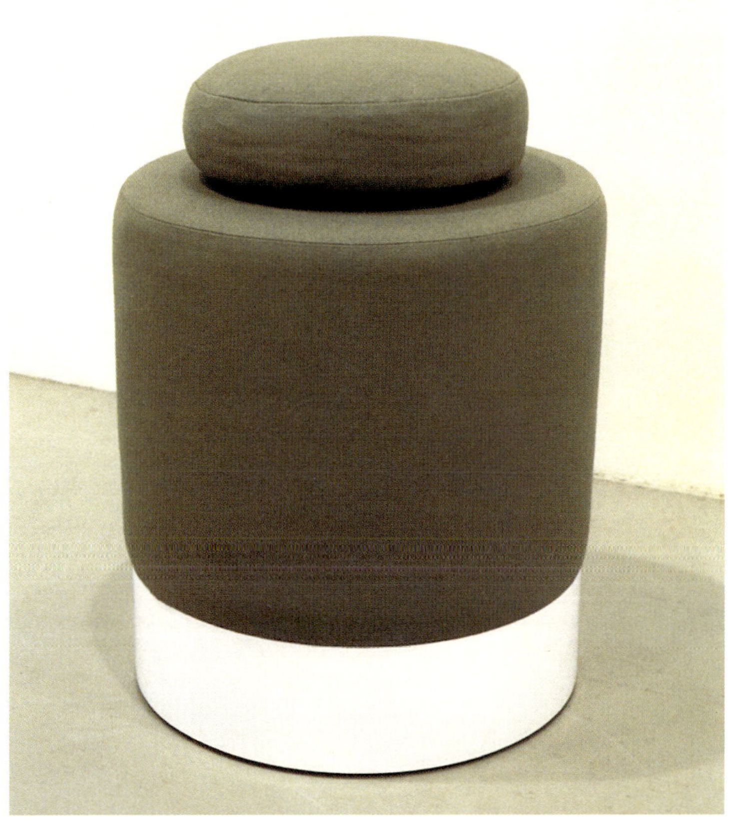

UNTITLED (UPHOLSTERED STOOL), 1997

such as the exposed china cabinets of the early art and Domestic days have been reinterpreted with patchy wood and cool white paint in the Would China Cabinet (1999), a diptych whose mirrored, repetitive, and perfectly executed forms aspire to high modern sculpture even as they address more worldly concerns. The fun McMakin has had with the visual and tactile pleasures of oversized or oddly turned knobs as found in earlier works such as the Cabinet for Slash's Office (1987) have been revisited in works like the Would Entry Table (1998), where a softball-sized knob invites touch and lightens one's mood. As these examples attest, wordplay has entered the design lexicon more emphatically for Domestic, as expressive uses of patchy wood fall under the category "Would" while reinterpretations of historical forms make up the "Knew" line, tweaking nostalgia and memory in witty ways.

The furniture more than ever aggressively toys with function, history, style, and expectation, something that can be attributed to McMakin's reinvigorated art practice, in which provocation and experimentation rule. The Knew Dresser (1999), for instance, appropriates Borax furniture styles of the 1940s in its vaguely deco curves and proportions but tries to hide these references under a shiny coat of white paint and fakes spatial depth with black shadows painted between mock legs. Circular white platforms humorously elevate the comfy Knew Swivel Wingback Chairs (1998) that dot the Getty offices, disengaging the legs from the floor in defiance of convention while introducing a new functionality.

The high level of craftsmanship that McMakin has been able to achieve in the Seattle workshop he established in 1998 derives from the dedicated group of furniture makers and finishers he has been able to recruit, coupled with the increasingly scarce, old-guard wood-

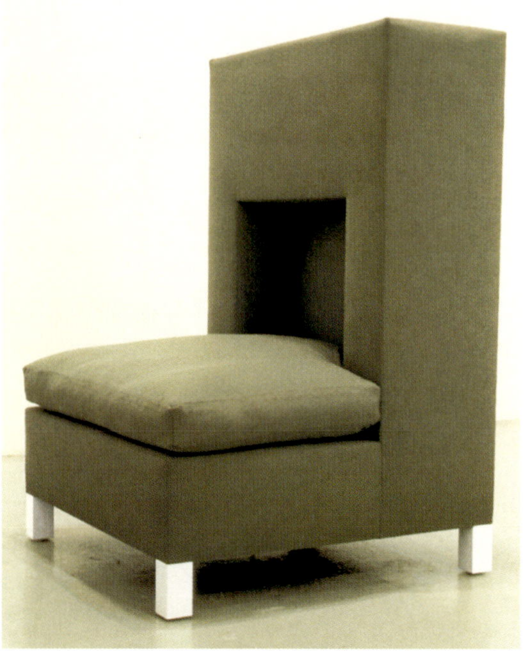

UNTITLED (UPHOLSTERED CHAIR), 1997
wool and painted wood
45 x 30 x 30 inches

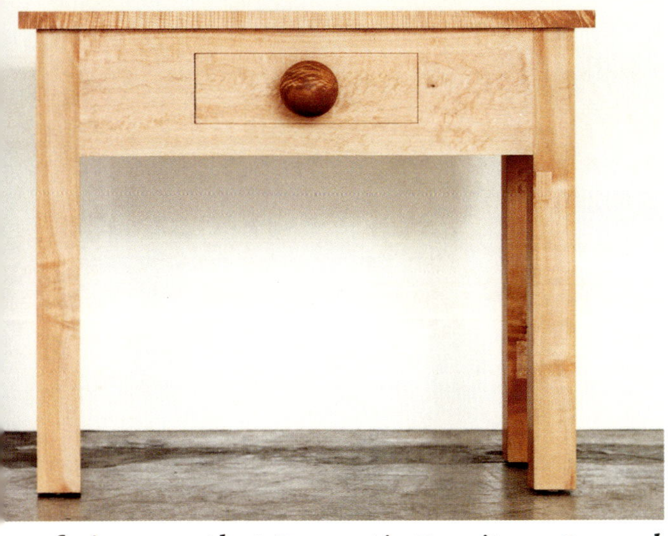

working techniques they use. His production manager Erik Aasen, one of the people who saw him through the Getty commission, helped to put together a team committed to realizing McMakin's vision. Members of this team bring their own strengths and expertise to the development of pieces so that Domestic Furniture Co. and Big Leaf Manufacturing, as the shop is called, are improved by their collaboration.

Ever since harboring desires to make furniture back in San Diego McMakin has longed for a top-level workshop, and with Big Leaf his dreams have come true. As a fine artist still inherently skeptical of the fetishization of craft over content, however, McMakin has found ways to ironically position his impeccably fashioned furniture. Thrift-store aesthetics have slyly filtered into McMakin's vocabulary in pieces such as his Writing Table and Chair (2000), whose perfect construction and finish are balanced by a sickly sweet coating of pink reminiscent of salvaged furniture refaced and repurposed by enterprising parents for a daughter's bedroom. Elsewhere, in pieces like the Dining Chest (1999) he designed for the renovation of the Berro Residence in Beverly Hills or the Swofford Chest of Drawers (2001) made for the Los Angeles Swofford Residence, off-kilter tints of green paint in the former and mixed-and-matched drawers and knobs in the latter suggest a loosening of quality control, even as one is hard-pressed to find a single flaw in the fabrication of either.

An endlessly mutable range of side chairs, activated by a wild array of fabric possibilities and wood finishes, have also erupted from the Domestic line, relying on a basic, iconic chair form derived from the lines of the old Cove Chair. These Fancy Chairs allow McMakin to play severe modernist,

WOULD ENTRY TABLE, 1998
oiled Big Leaf maple
34 x 40 x 18 inches

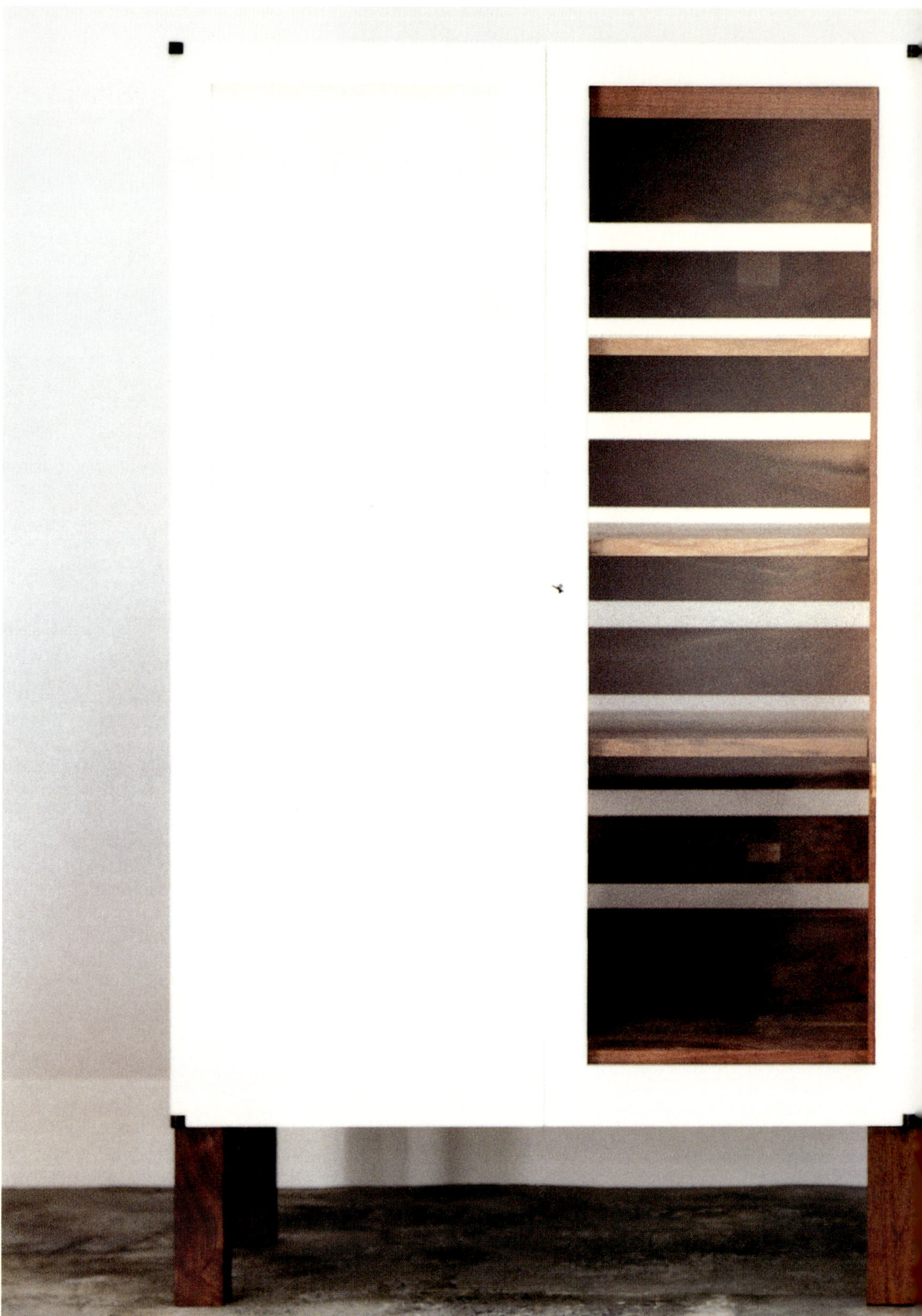

WOULD CHINA CABINET, 1999

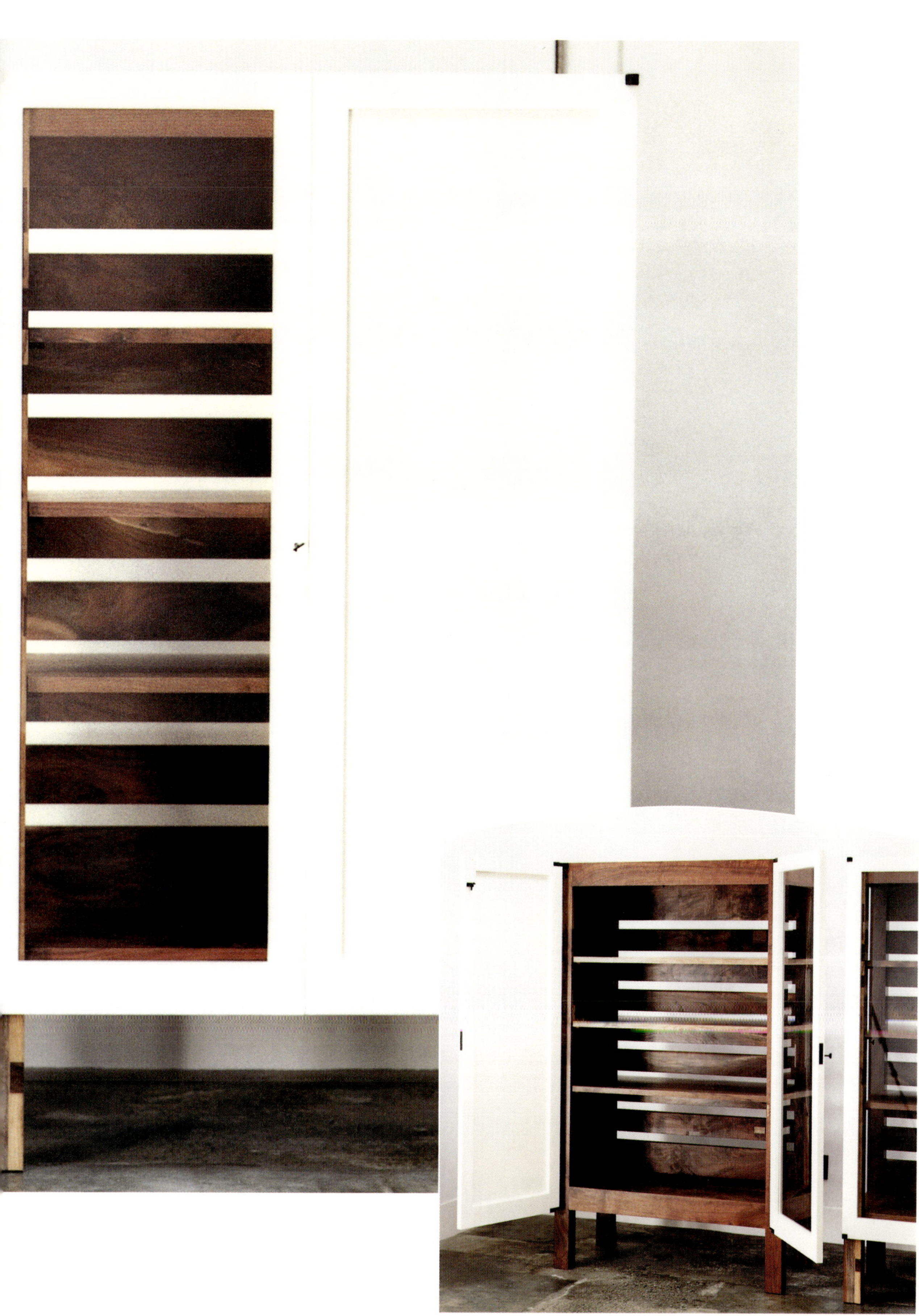

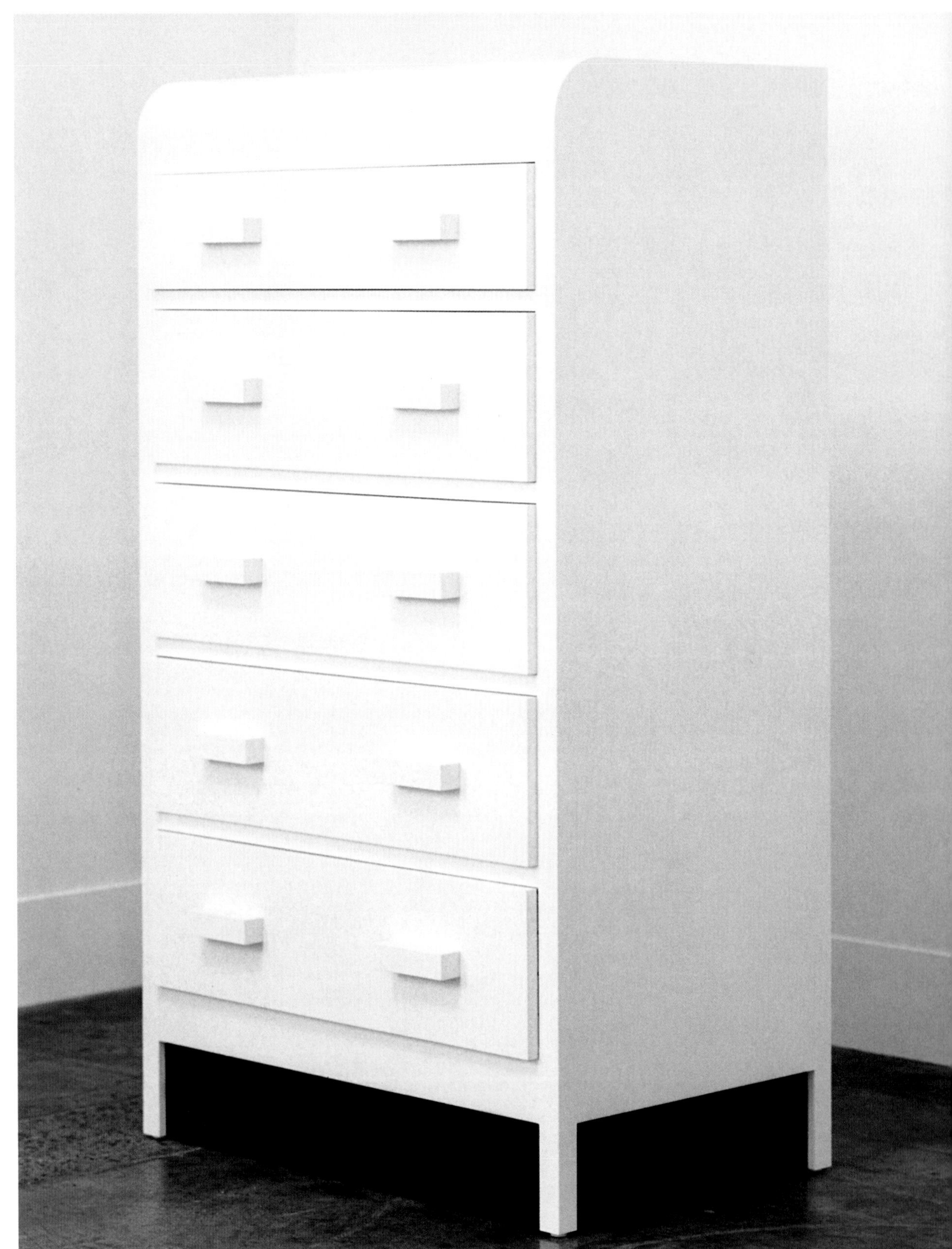

KNEW DRESSER, 1999

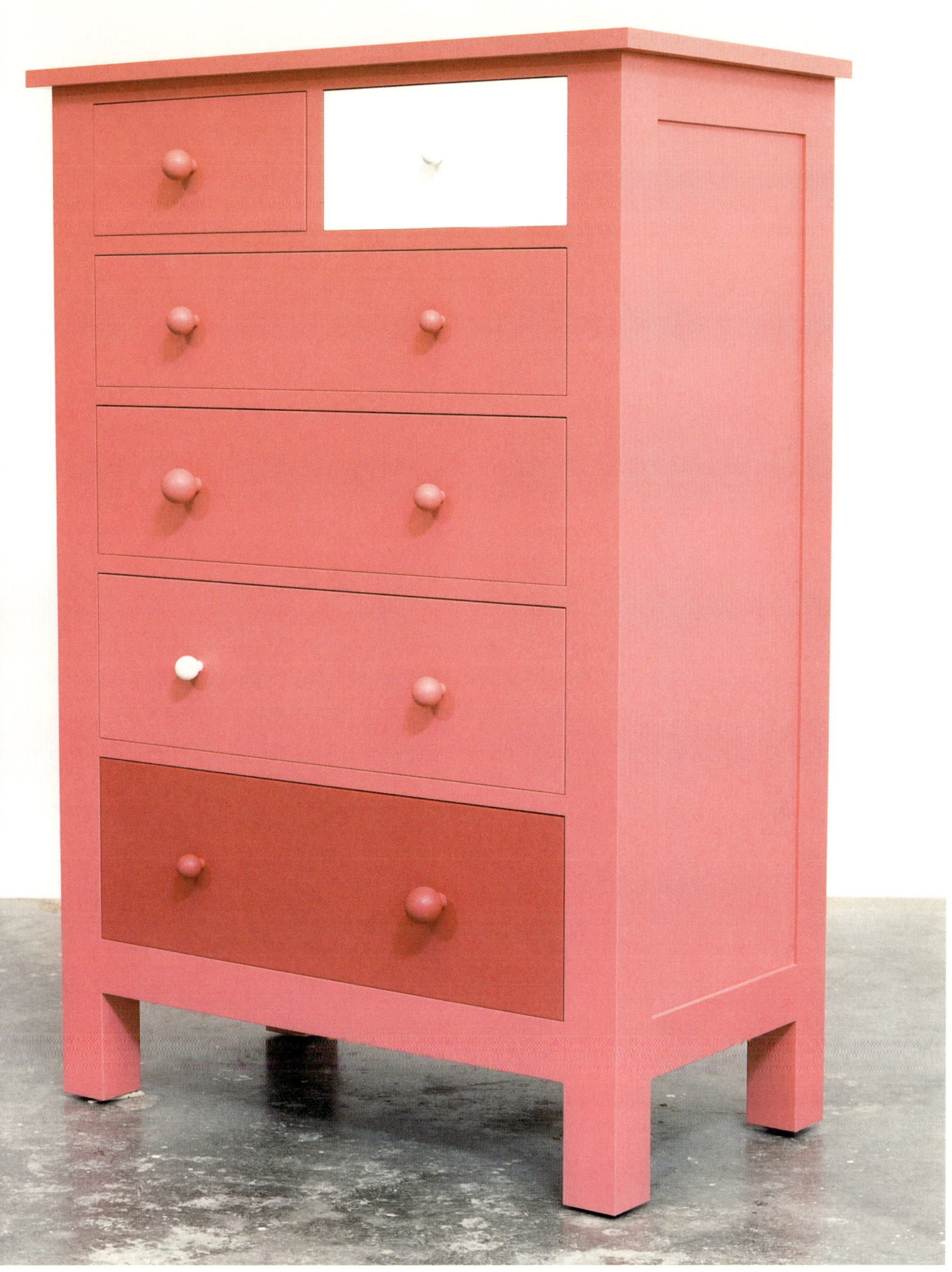

SWOFFORD CHEST OF DRAWERS, 2001
painted wood
56 x 38 x 21 inches

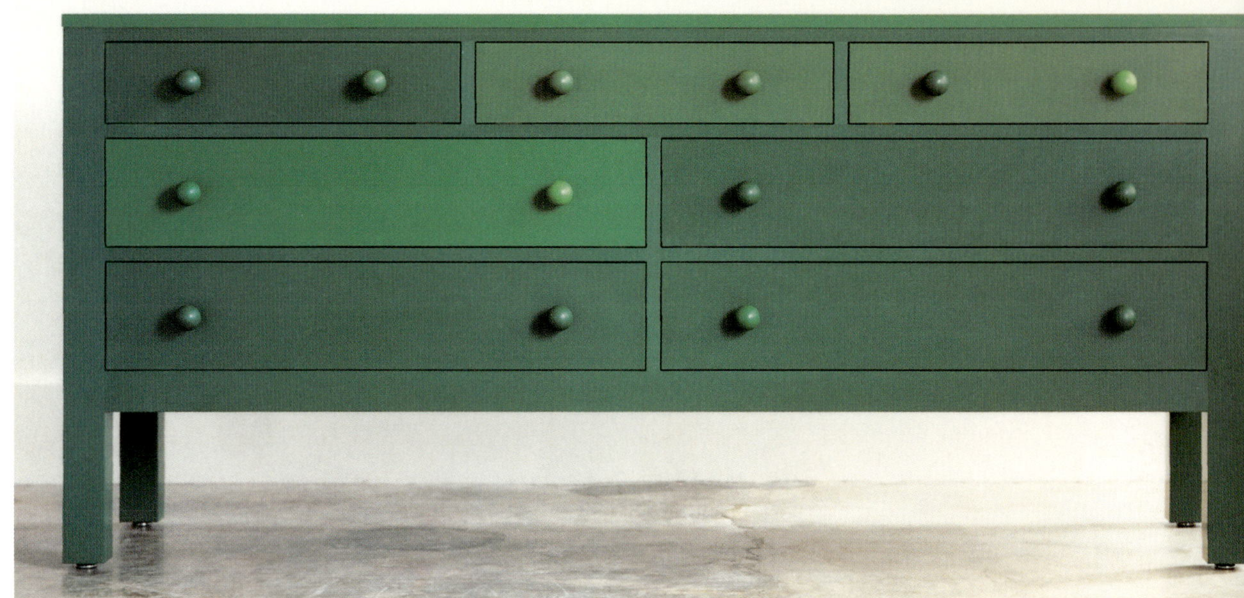

DINING CHEST, 1999
painted eastern maple
40 x 88 x 24 inches

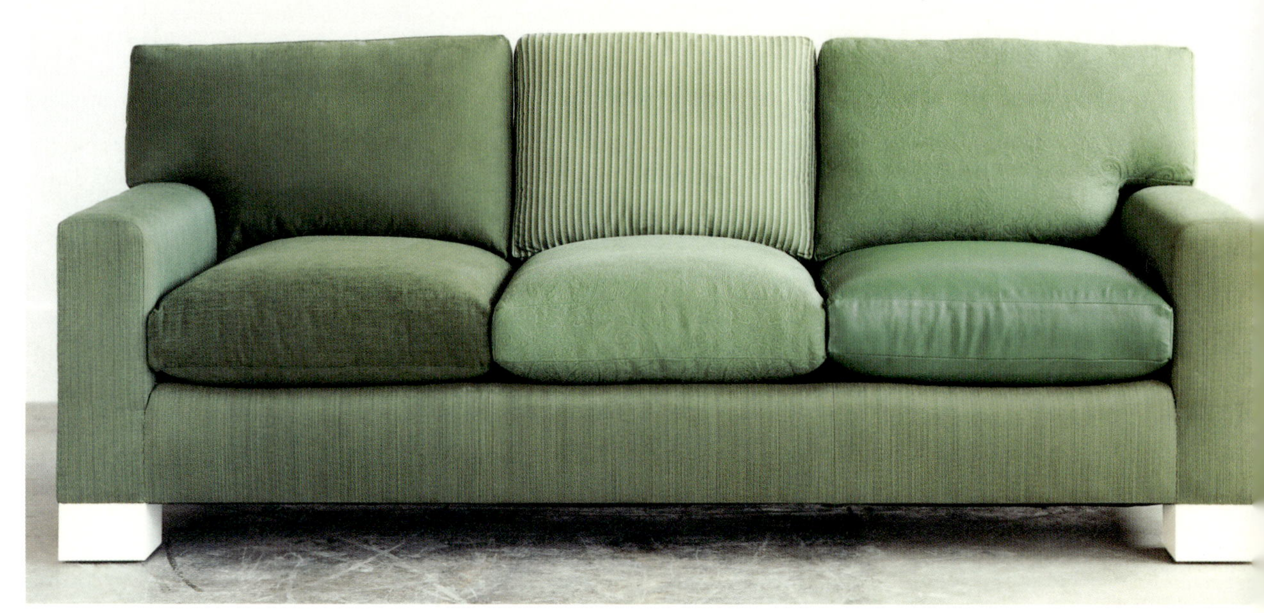

LOOSE BACK SOFA, 1999
mixed media
36 x 84 x 40 inches

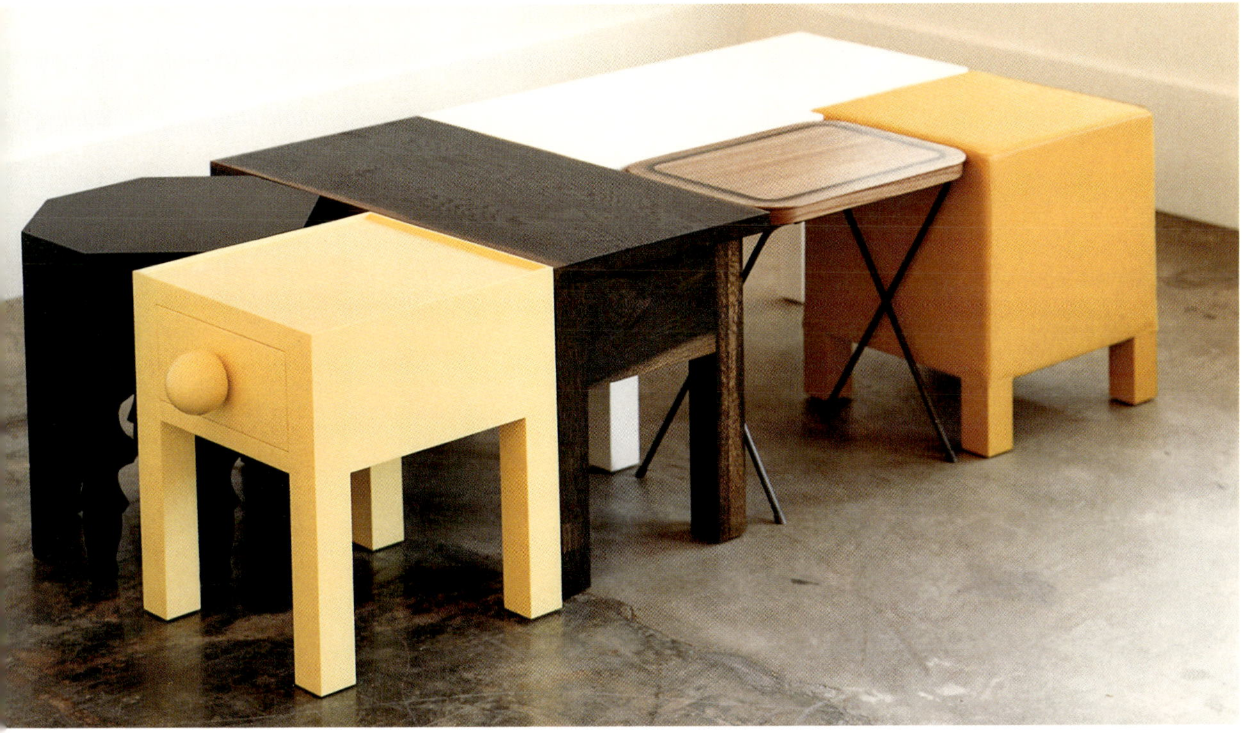

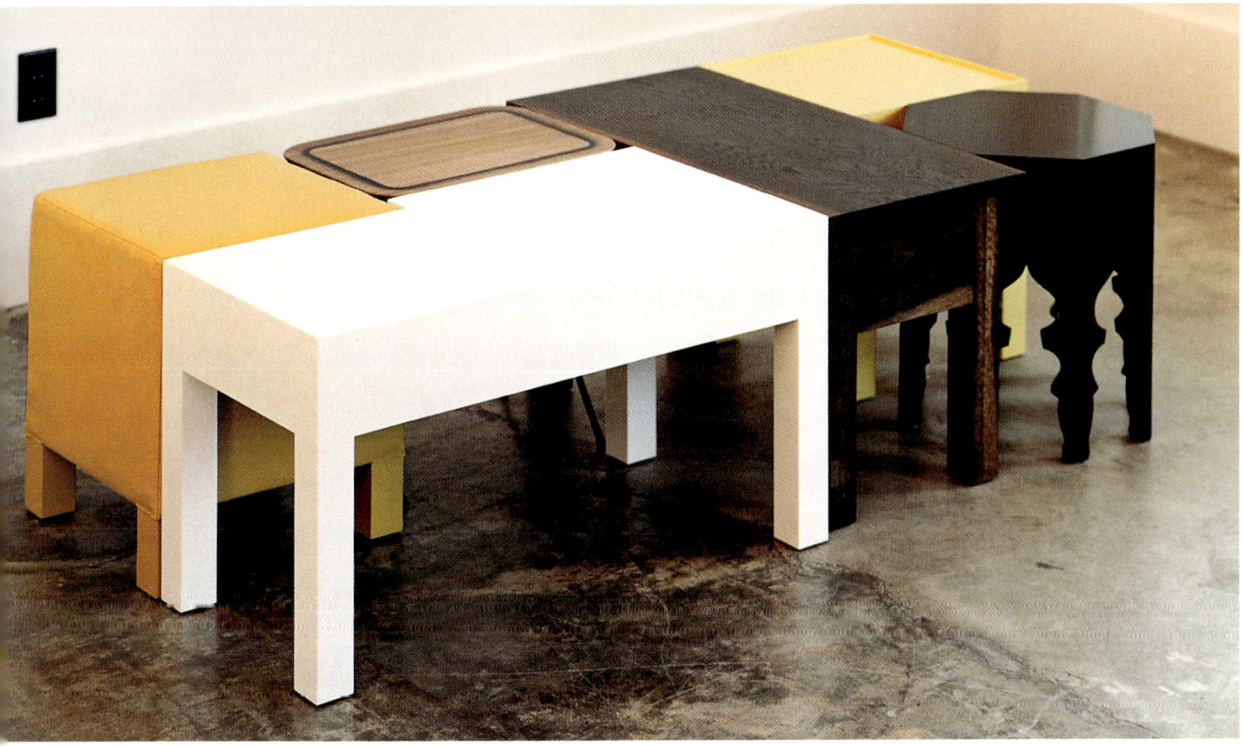

LIGHT COFFEE TABLE, 2000

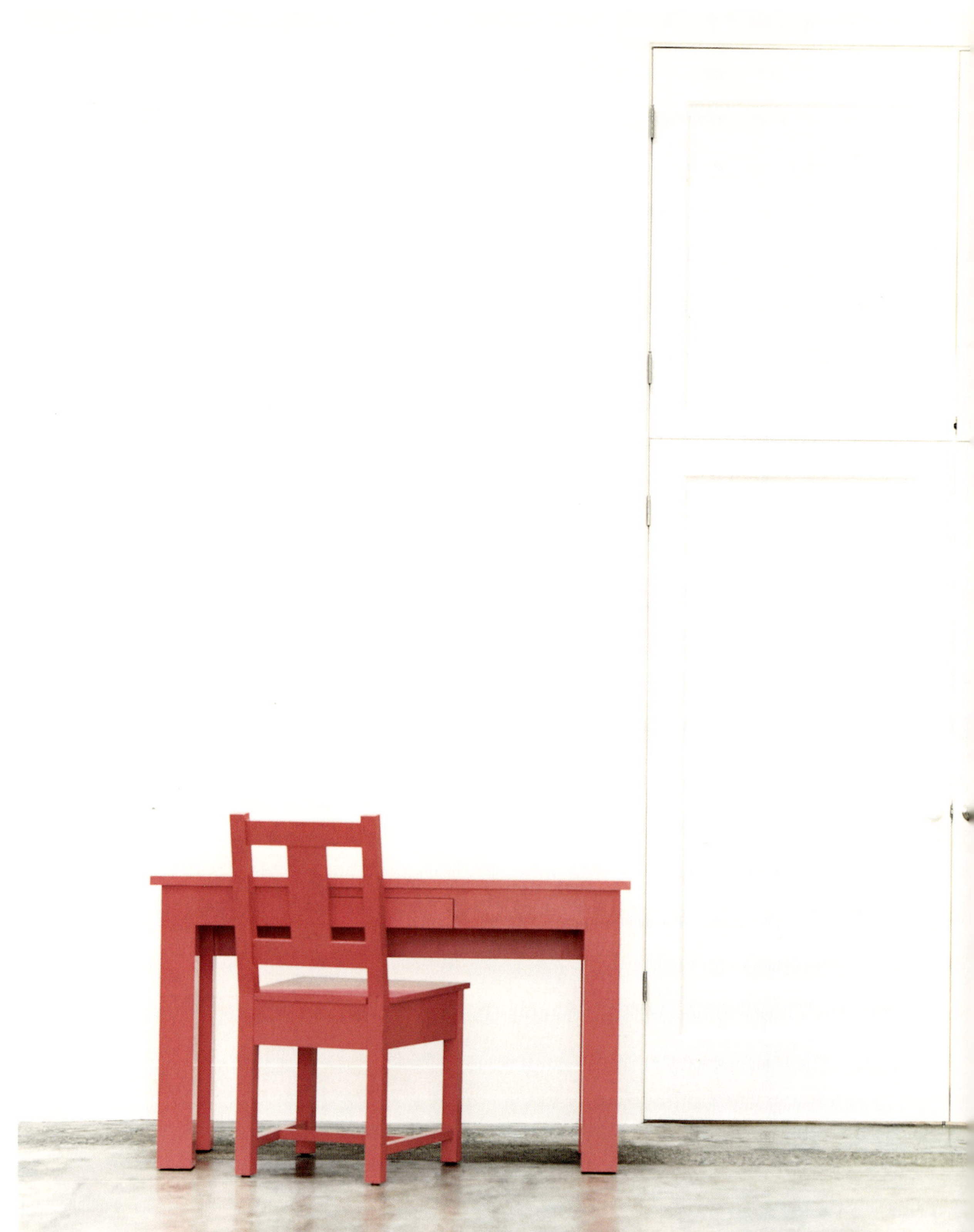

WRITING TABLE AND CHAIR, 2000

country decorator, empire stylist, or deco dilettante with ease, sometimes mixing a whole range of styles to make unpretentious groupings. Such fabric mixes have also appeared in larger upholstered items such as the Loose Back Sofa (1999), achieving a blend of elegance and funkiness that is remarkably adaptable to a range of personal tastes or architectural modes. One of the artist's most exemplary confabulations of periods and styles was let loose in a coffee table for the Light Residence in Marin County (2000) that comprises six table-like forms of uniform height but differing shapes, colors, and materials. When placed together, a 1950s-style TV table, hexagonal Moorish stand, yellow ottoman, white bench, patchy ebonied oak bench, and yellow nightstand form a long rectangular surface at perfect coffee-table height, albeit one deliriously schizophrenic in stylistic and formal identity. Although it appears to be cobbled together from flea-market finds, each piece reveals itself to be exquisitely custom-crafted, and the intention of the gesture ultimately becomes crystal clear. Increasingly, it is commissions such as this that allow the full breadth of McMakin's design acumen to show, bringing out his finely honed intuitions about stylistic appropriateness, the meaning and uses of decoration, and pragmatic problem-solving. In projects such as those for the aforementioned Benedek, Bloomberg, and Berro residences to renovations for the Rhodes, Murkoff, Wright, Ghez, and Jones families and the Sea Level offices, inventive furnishings and architectural concepts seem to pour from his pen, drawing an ever-widening circle of decorative modes to make his own.

While his taste has always been unerringly classic, marked by an eye for proportion and a scrupulous avoidance of trends, McMakin has often found inspiration in the tacky and outré. He cites the campy technicolor film *The Music Man* (1962) as a central inspiration (as much for its nimble wordplay as its neo-Victorian look) and counts the Hollywood Empire architecture of John Woolf, for whom a door really was adornment, as a longtime favorite. In *The Music Man*, certain words have been singled out for scrutiny and embellishment in a way not dissimilar to McMakin's

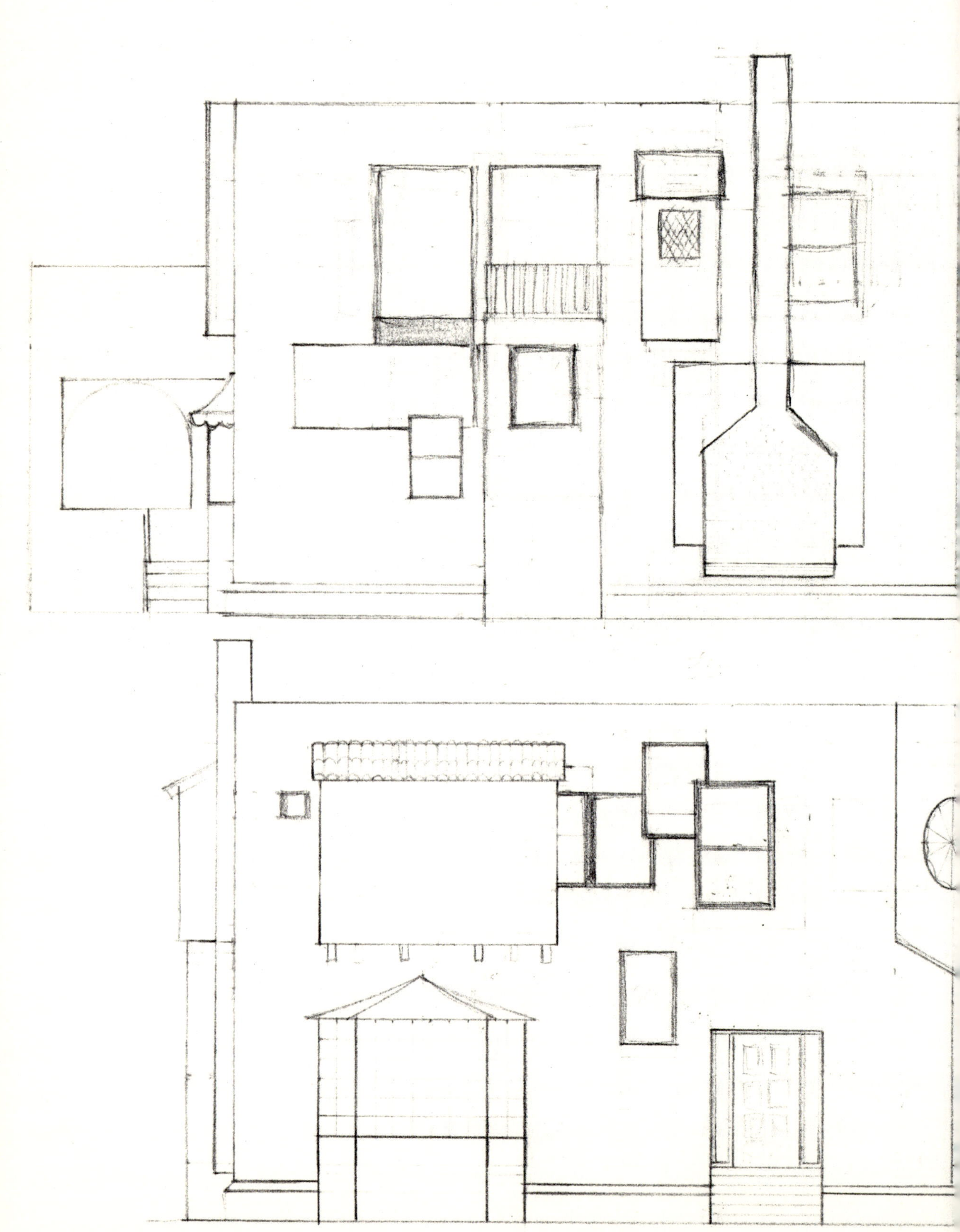

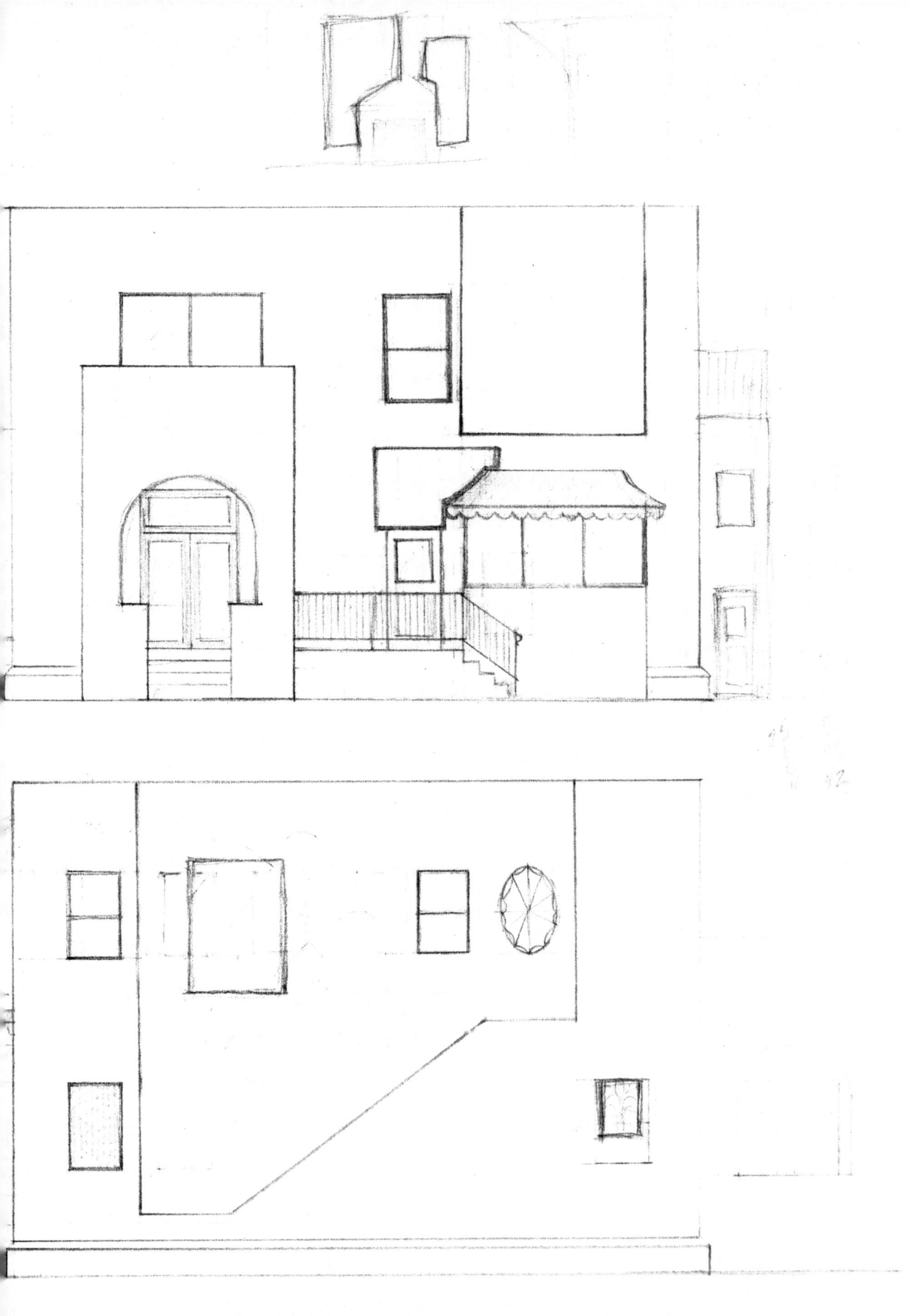

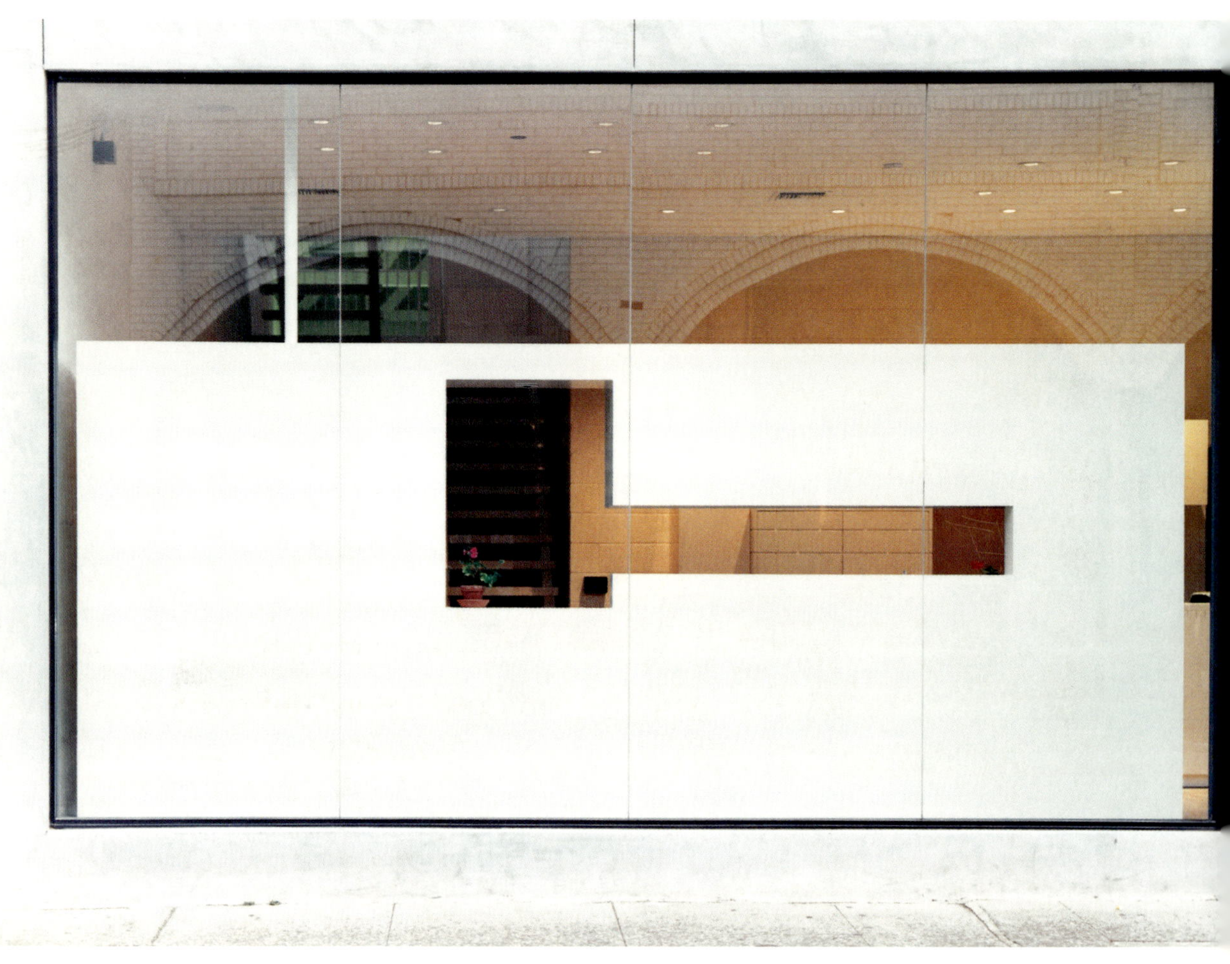

SEA LEVEL FAÇADE, VENICE, CALIFORNIA, 1998

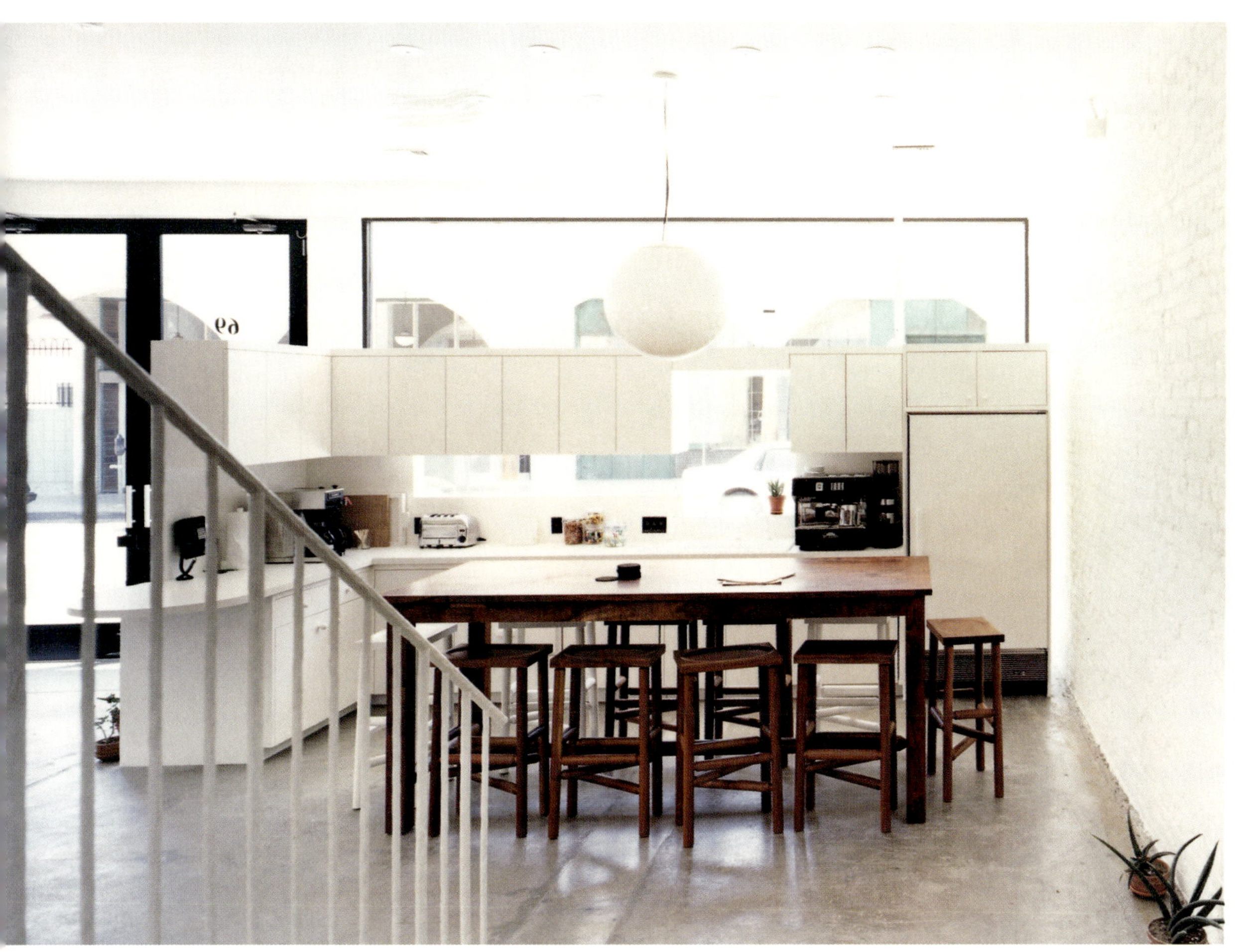

SEA LEVEL KITCHEN, VENICE, CALIFORNIA, 1998

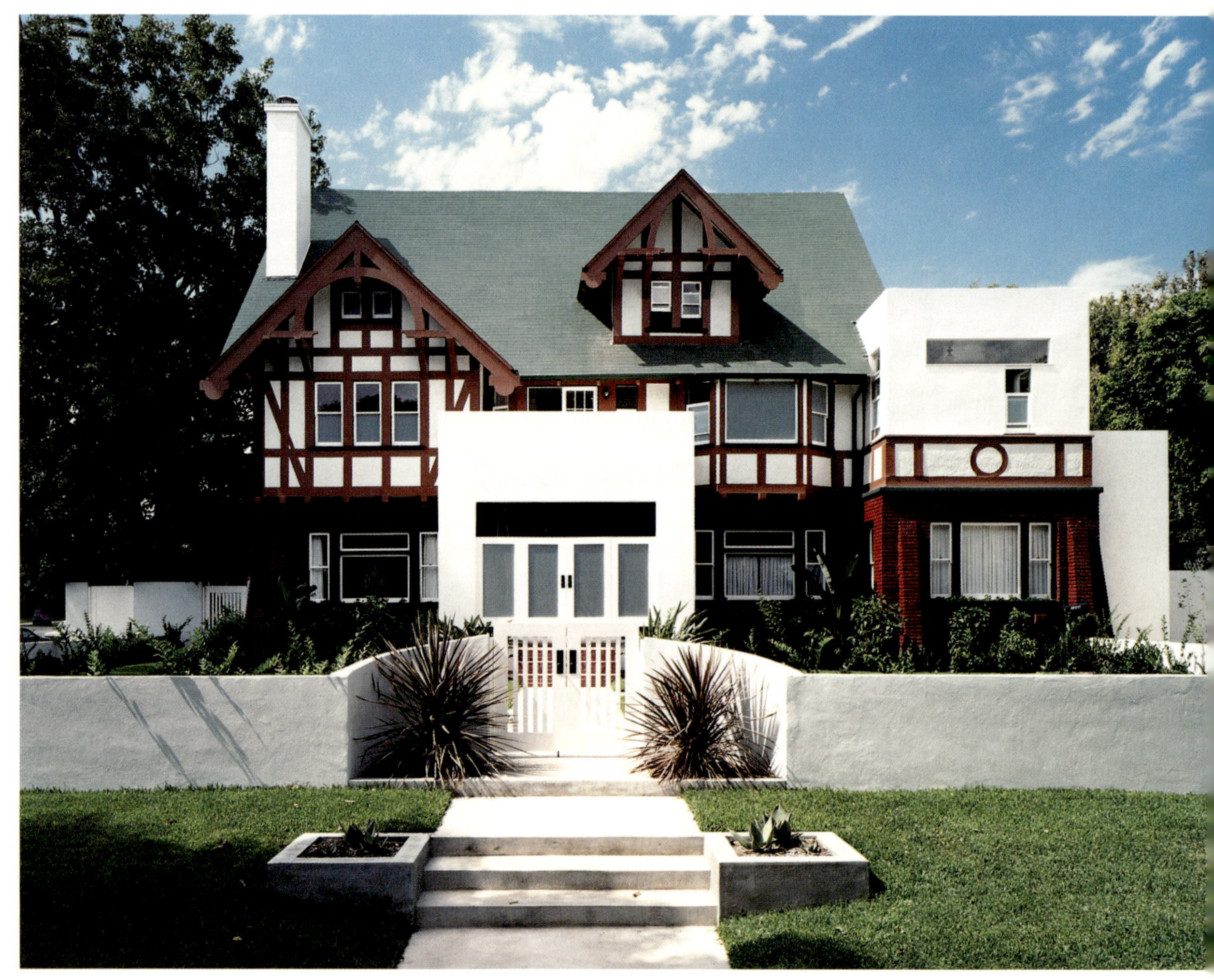

BERRO RESIDENCE FAÇADE, BEVERLY HILLS, CALIFORNIA, 2000

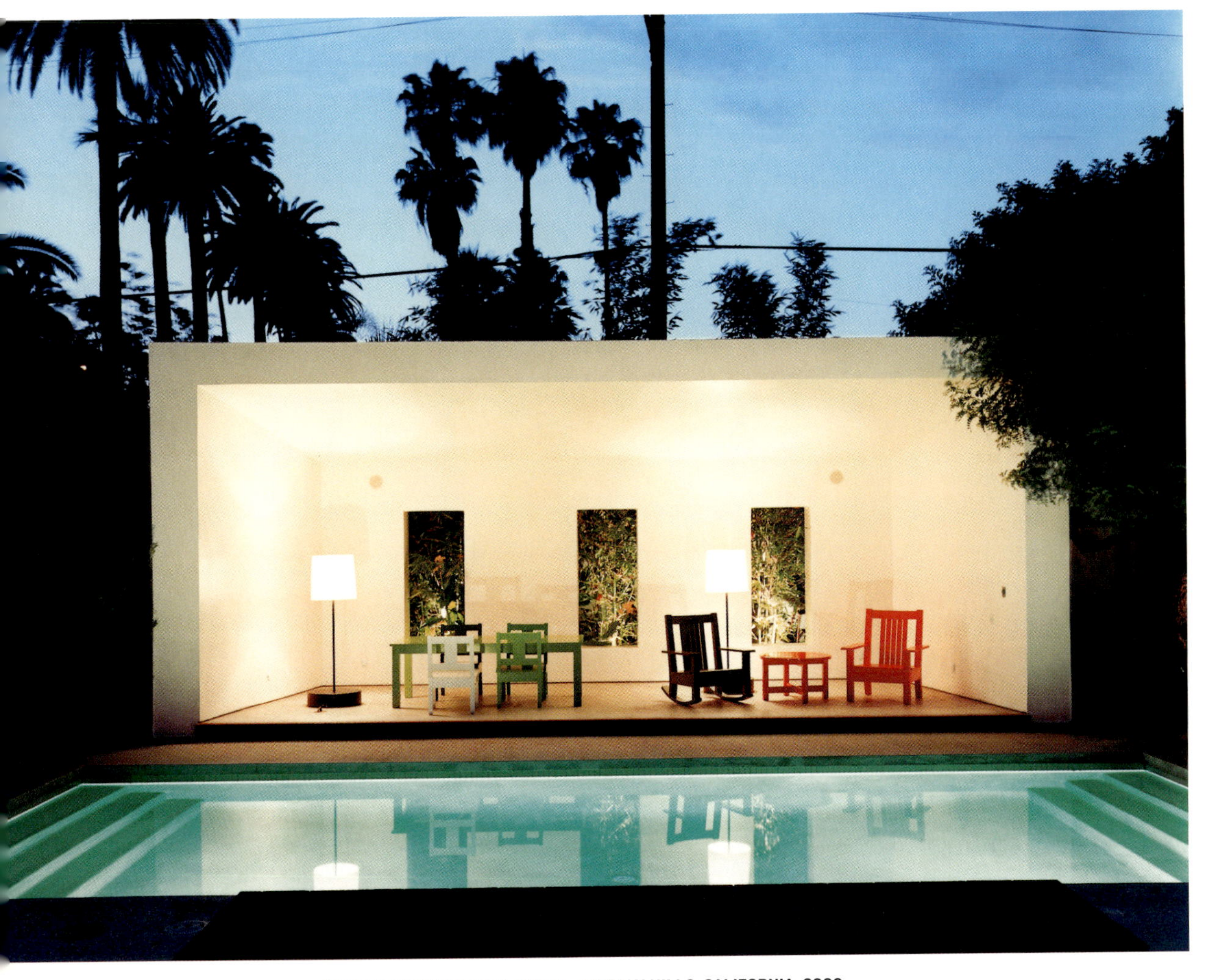

BERRO RESIDENCE POOL HOUSE, BEVERLY HILLS, CALIFORNIA, 2000

treatment of furniture or art objects. Moreover, the film's setting, River City, embodies the kind of fictitious memory that his furniture and art have also often employed.[11] In fact, for the exhibition at The Museum of Contemporary Art, Los Angeles (MOCA), McMakin has built a room of furnishings based entirely upon memories of his grandparents' house in Oklahoma. Titled *Lequita Faye Melvin* (2003), the sort of name one might find in a movie though belonging to his mother who grew up in the house, it underlines the constant guide that memory has played in his practice. Also in the MOCA exhibition is a wall of standard white refrigerators, created by laying them on their side in a running bond pattern. Simulating a brick wall, but with a grossly exaggerated scale and an obviously domestic referent, this installation was first realized in an exhibition at the Seattle Art Museum in 1999 and relates to McMakin's long-standing interest in refrigerators as the center of the home and nexus of family nourishment, both physically and psychologically.[12] Other artworks incorporating refrigerator references have also appeared over the years, including *Two-Sided Shelving Unit with Painting* (2000), which slyly ignores the refrigerator in its title but evokes it unequivocally in form.

One of his latest enthusiasms has been for the ad-hoc agglomerations characterizing hippie building practices of the late 1960s and early 70s, where mix-and-match scrap wood, organic accretions of rooms, and a fondness for burls and backwoods sites amounted to a verifiable aesthetic.[13] When channeled through his own reductivist sensibility, aided by references to other types of folk art as well as the work of master craftsman George Nakashima, the hippie look is much transformed but still goes a long way toward explaining the profusion of patches in pieces like Would Side Table Extra Patchy (1999) or the peekaboo burl panels in the Jones Master Bed (2001). One might even discern an ahead-of-the-curve hillbilly modernism in some of McMakin's latest work, inspired by the wobbly do-it-yourself-ism of American Windsor chairs and their downriver progeny. His Dawn's Desk Chair (2001) is the exemplar here, affecting the off-kilter and constantly-

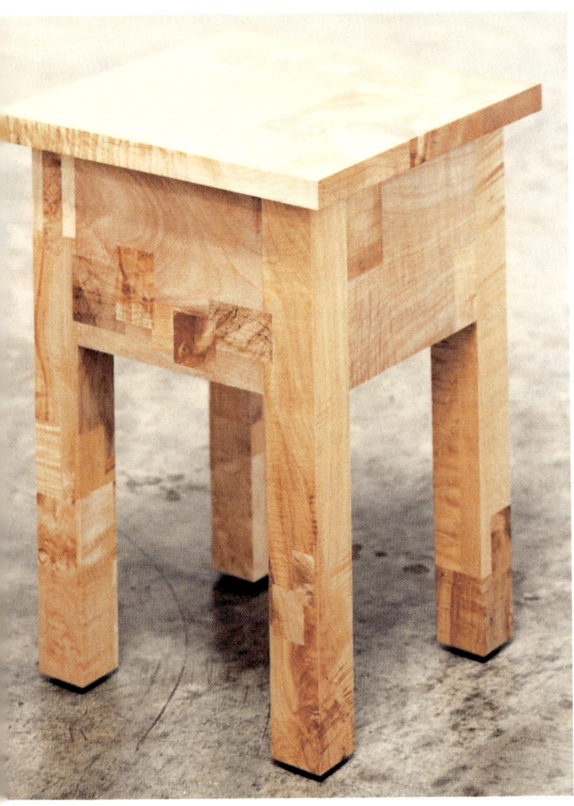

under-repair look of an Appalachian porch furnishing, complete with signature McMakin hobo patches. However, the Domestic Furniture version made from luminous white holly sits squarely on the floor, every millimeter of its surface smoothed to a downy softness. This ironic masterpiece of high-craft craftlessness has spawned a low end-table/stool cousin and was also produced with a related bookshelf that has the sort of tacked-on decorative molding that exemplified middlebrow taste in the first half of the twentieth century.

If anything can be said about McMakin's current predilections, it is that the whole world of style and decoration has become of interest to him. He has come to the conclusion that decoration and ornament are tantamount to expressions of love and compassion, and that all stylistic modes are capable of expressing as much. His discovery in the early 1990s of the writings of art historian Oleg Grabar helped him toward this realization, assuaging his long-standing modernist/minimalist fears of the decorative.[14] Grabar has written persuasively about the functions of ornament and decoration, which can be categorized by different styles. McMakin has taken many of these ideas to heart. The completion of a building could be said to hinge upon the hanging of a door. That act of completion, of tying together the constituent parts to make a whole, is quite akin to impulses of adornment and ornamentation as found, say, in the realm of fashion. Across many cultures Grabar has found surprising connections between understandings of ornament, all of which could be said to mirror McMakin's

WOULD SIDE TABLE EXTRA PATCHY, 1999

dogged attention to furniture as a crucial and eloquent feature of our collective lives:

> A wise medieval Jewish saying from the Book of Ben Sirach goes as follows: "A mind settled on an intelligent thought is like the stucco decoration on the wall of a colonnade." The contemplation of something intelligent is compared to what makes a wall beautiful, that is something plastered on it...Decoration seems to complete an object, a wall or a person, by providing it with quality.[15]

Grabar then turns further East for another example:

> the Sanskrit word *bhusati*...means "to adorn." It too implies the successful completion of an act, of an object, or even of a state of mind or soul. In being applied to the adornment of women, it means the prosperity of the male head of a family or of a household. For a king in battle, the word denotes the sound and sight of his victory, just as it can be an attribute of copulation, which perfects a union in creating life. And, in a most beautiful image, the moon is the adornment of the night, because, without it, the night is incomplete.[16]

Such a sense of the importance of ornament has been latent in McMakin's work from the beginning, first evidenced in the hand-painted surfaces of his furniture tableaux, then in his embrace of the human urge to display objects on top of furnishings (what Grabar would see as "completion"), until it reached full flowering in the more overtly decorative late-Domestic period. Likewise, McMakin relished the thought that Gill, himself a student of the ornamentalist Louis Sullivan, felt his white-stucco walls were not complete until they were covered with the organic decoration of creeping vines or bougainvillea.[17]

McMakin has taken an equal-opportunity view of ornament, training his eye on quintessentially modern elements such as the pendant lamp for both sculptural and functional (read "art" and "furniture") pieces, or to modular case goods in artworks such as *Double Chest with Contrasting Drawers* (2000). He has incorporated vaguely Asian motifs in works such as

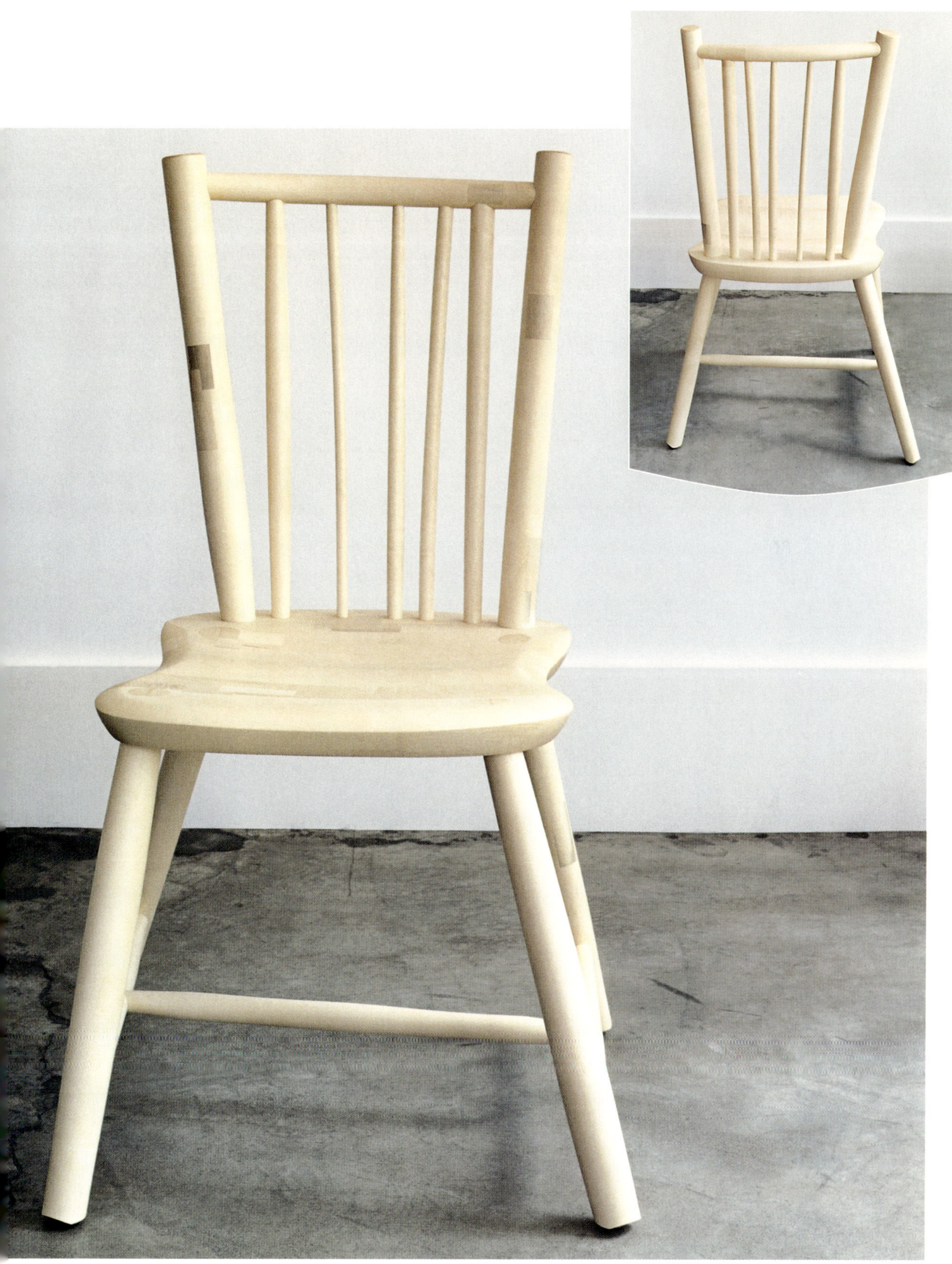

DAWN'S DESK CHAIR, 2001

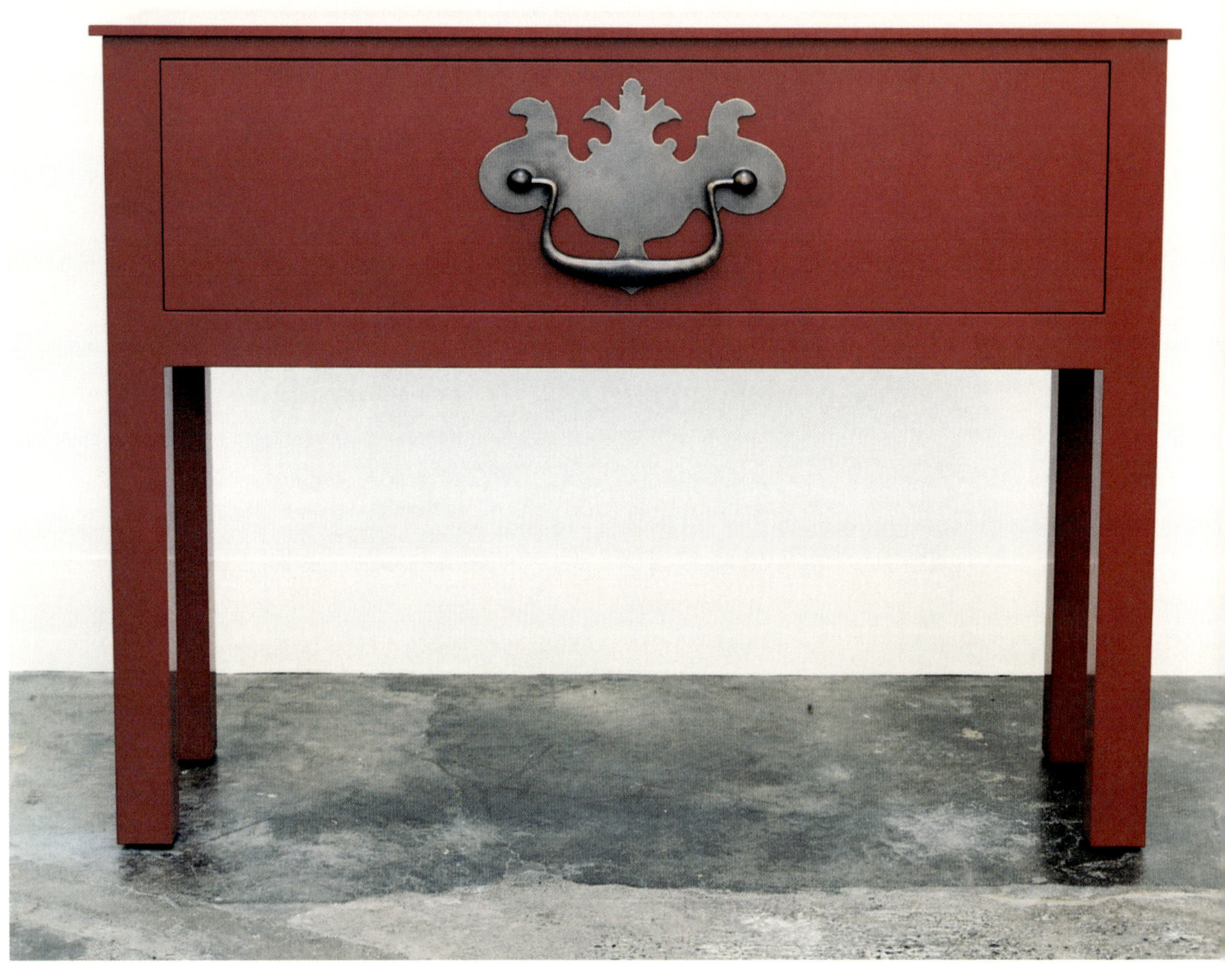

JONES ENTRY TABLE, 2001
painted eastern maple and bronze
38 x 48 x 16 inches

the Petra/Wong Breakfast Room Server (2000) or Jones Entry Table (2001), and dabbled with Middle Eastern standards such as in the Dan Moroccan Side Table (1996). His recent incorporation of enameled metal tabletops has him sidling up to more commercial or specialized furniture-design idioms that harken back to the earlier twentieth century, while a new object utilizing this same material, the Enamel-Top Table (2001), has more contemporary and prosaic roots. While it reads like a typically cool, clean McMakin design, it was tangentially inspired by the round plastic "tables" pizza-delivery restaurants put inside their boxes to avoid squashing the product in transit. Because of their diminutive scale and obvious referent, McMakin has dubbed this early-twenty-first-century niche product a "Barbie Table." When placed into the stylish environment the first Enamel-Top Table was intended for, many guests would likely fail to recognize the allusion and instead be content to admire its beautiful proportions and finish. Most of McMakin's work is like that: tasteful, stylish, and well-built furniture that enriches the homes it inhabits. However, those willing to spend time looking at McMakin's designs find his pieces slowly asserting themselves into their consciousness until each comes into its own as an eloquent contributor to the exciting enactment of everyday life. Figure and ground become indistinguishable — a door is not just a portal but an all-important, completing adornment.

NOTES

1 Roy McMakin, quoted in Michael Darling, "Domesticating Art," *L.A. Weekly* 20, no. 4, 19–25 December 1997, 43.
2 Conversation with the author, 20 May 2002.
3 Conversation with the author, 13 August 2001.
4 McMakin, quoted in "Domesticating Art," 43.
5 Conversation with the author, 13 August 2001.
6 McMakin, quoted in "Domesticating Art," 43.
7 Conversation with the author, 13 August 2001.
8 Brian O'Doherty, "Inside the White Cube: Notes on the Gallery Space, Part I," *Artforum* 14, no. 7 (March 1976): 25.
9 Conversation with the author, 20 May 2002.
10 Mark Wigley, *White Walls, Designer Dresses: The Fashioning of Modern Architecture* (Cambridge, Mass.: The MIT Press, 1995), xiv.
11 Conversation with the author, 20 May 2002.
12 Ibid.
13 See Art Boericke, *Handmade Houses: A Guide to the Woodbutcher's Art* (San Francisco: Scrimshaw Press, 1973) for an eye-opening introduction to the genre.
14 Conversation with the author, 20 May 2002.
15 Oleg Grabar, *The Mediation of Ornament*, Bollingen Series, v. 38 (Washington, D.C.: The National Gallery of Art; and Princeton, N.J.: Princeton University Press, 1992), 25.
16 Ibid., 26.
17 Conversation with the author, 20 May 2002.

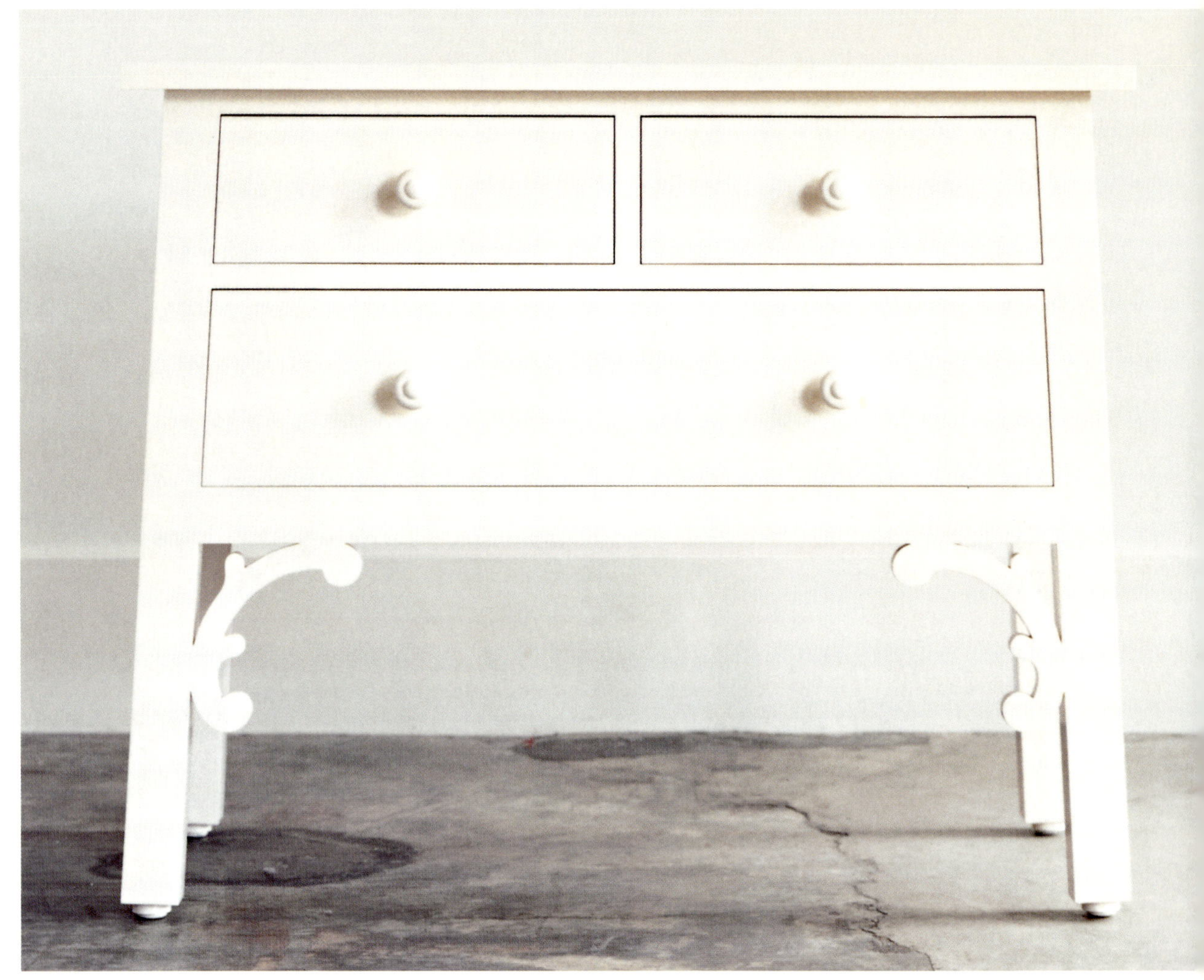

PETRA/WONG BREAKFAST ROOM SERVER, 2000

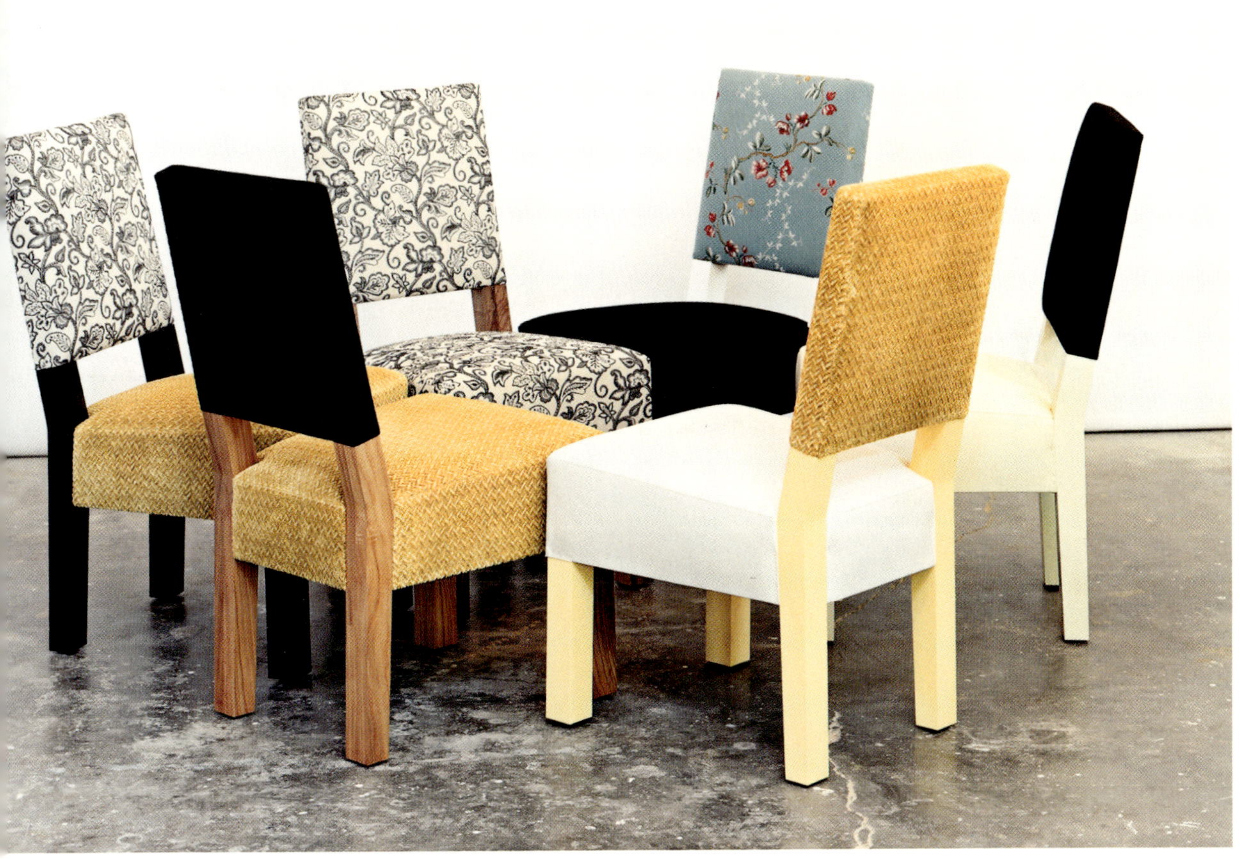

SWOFFORD FANCY CHAIRS, 2001
mixed media
38 x 19 x 23 inches each

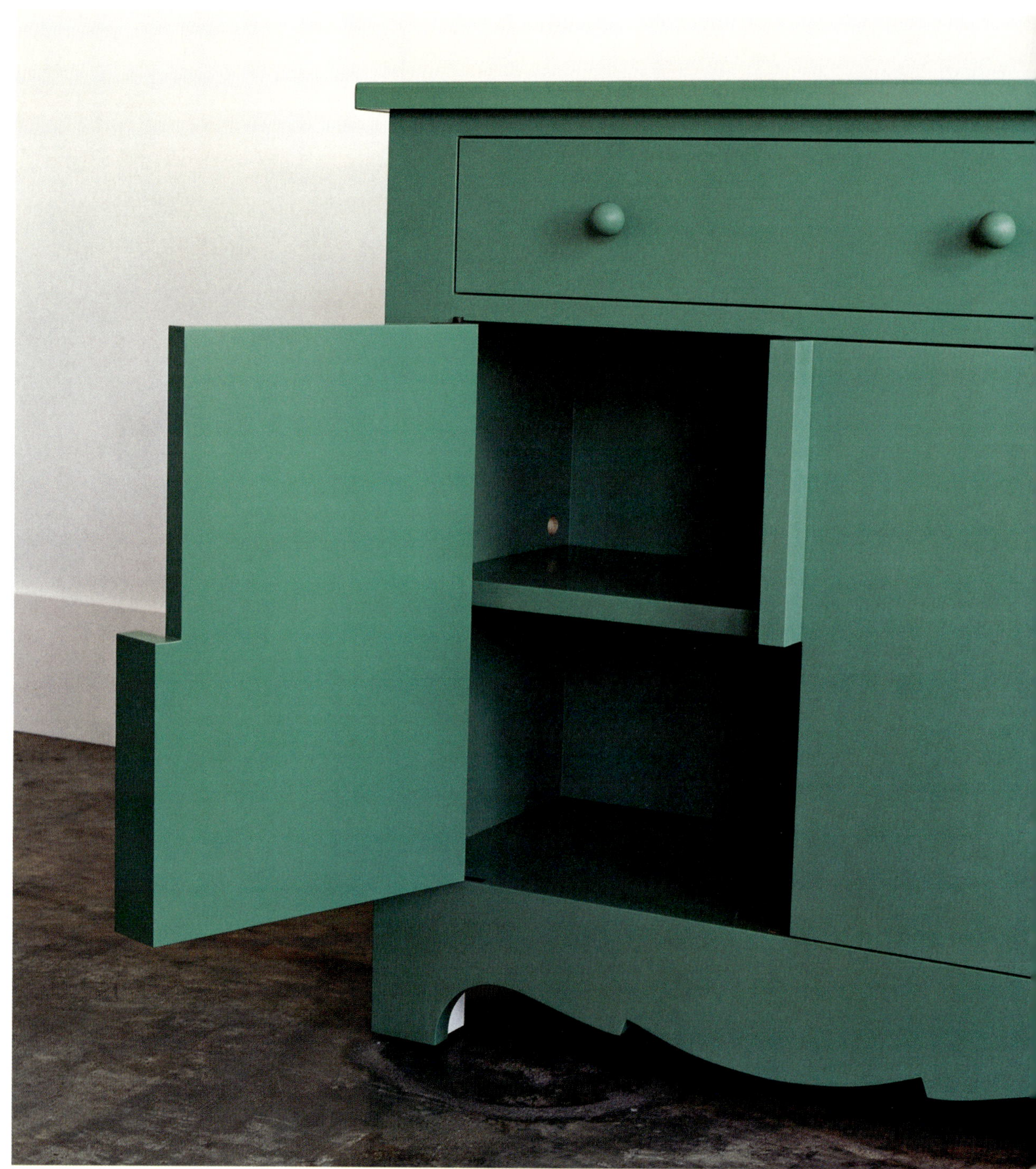

KITCHEN CASE, 2001
painted eastern maple with enamel top
38 x 36 x 17 inches

CHECKLIST

UNTITLED, 1979
mixed media
dimensions variable
collection of the artist, Seattle

SELF-PORTRAIT WITH JIM, 1981
gouache on paper
13 x 16 inches
collection of the artist, Seattle

UNTITLED from **A HOUSE, 1982**
gouache on paper
13 x 16 inches
ection of Kelly and Pam McMakin, San Diego

UNTITLED from **INSIDE, 1982**
maple
40¾ x 35½ x 20 inches
collection of the artist, Seattle

UNTITLED (SERVER), 1983
pigmented varnish and acrylic on maple
41¾ x 49 x 18 inches
collection of the artist, Seattle

from **ROY MELVIN'S DEATH, 1984**
ting: acrylic on panel; table: enamel on maple
ng: 18 x 12 inches; table: 27½ x 15¾ x 15¾ inches
collection of the artist, Seattle; and
Museum of Contemporary Art, San Diego

from **AN INFORMAL DINING ROOM SET, 1985**
painted wood
37 x 19 x 15 inches
collection of the artist, Seattle

NEW TABLE, 1985
und table with lacquer on solid core plywood
29½ x 19 x 27½ inches
ection of Anne and Robert Nugent, San Diego

UNTITLED, 1985–86
color photographs
three photographs; 10¾ x 13¾ inches each
collection of the artist, Seattle

NTITLED (SHORTENED ARCH TABLE), 1985
nahogany and enamel on solid core plywood
34 x 34 x 17 inches
ection of Anne and Robert Nugent, San Diego

BROOKE'S DEATH, 1986
wood and paint
52 x 38 x 20 inches
collection of the artist, Seattle

HUGH DAVIES CREDENZA, 1986
painted wood
36 x 84 x 21 inches
Museum of Contemporary Art, San Diego

MISCELLANEOUS DRAWINGS, 1986–2001
pencil and ink on paper
dimensions variable
collection of the artist, Seattle

TRILLING SIDEBOARD, 1986
oil on wood
40 x 40 x 16 inches
collection of Mark Trilling

UNTITLED (BLACK OTTOMAN), 1986/2002
upholstery and wood
26 x 60 x 30 inches
collection of Spot Welders, Venice

UNTITLED (CABINET), 1986
maple and solid core plywood
66 x 28 x 22 inches
collection of Elvi Olesen, San Diego

UNTITLED (GREEN OTTOMAN), 1986
upholstery and wood
34½ x 35½ x 21½ inches
collection of the artist, Seattle

A DRESSER, 1987
maple plywood
49 x 38 x 19 inches
collection of Mark Trilling

CABINET FOR SLASH'S OFFICE, 1987
maple and maple plywood
38 x 36 x 17 inches
collection of Mark Trilling

COVE TABLE, 1987
maple plywood
16 x 19 x 19 inches
collection of Steven Jensen

MAHOGANY CHEST, 1987
mahogany
61 x 40 x 24¾ inches
collection of Anne and Robert Nugent, San Diego

MISCELLANEOUS DESIGN OBJECTS, 1987–2001
mixed media
dimensions variable
collection of the artist, Seattle

PROTOTYPE COVE CHAIR, 1987
maple plywood
35 x 18 x 15 inches
collection of Anne and Robert Nugent, San Diego

CHINA CABINET, c. 1988
maple plywood and glass
approximately 72 x 40 x 18 inches
courtesy of Domestic Furniture Co., Seattle

ARCHITECTURAL PROJECTS, 1989–2002
color photographs
11 x 14 inches each
courtesy of Domestic Furniture Co., Seattle

BIG CHAIR, 1989
wool grospoint upholstery and wood
40 x 39 x 37 inches
private collection

CAUDAL BENCH, 1989
maple plywood
17 x 36 x 18 inches
collection of Steven Jensen, Los Angeles

STANWYCK PEDESTAL SIDE TABLE, 1989
painted wood
22 x 18 x 18 inches
Benedek Collection, Santa Monica

MAPLE CHEST, 1990
maple and maple plywood
61 x 41 x 22½ inches
collection of Anne and Robert Nugent, San Diego

OVAL COFFEE TABLE, 1990
maple
18 x 65 x 25 inches
courtesy of Domestic Furniture Co., Seattle

second version of **SIMPLE CHAIR, 1990**
spruce with waxed finish
36 x 22 x 19 inches
collection of the artist, Seattle

SILVER TABLE, 1991
cast iron with silver plating
9 x 17 x 11 inches
collection of the artist, Seattle

ROSENBERG OTTOMAN, 1993
upholstery and wood
16 x 12 x 24 inches
Rosenberg Collection, Los Angeles

SOPHISTICATED WINGBACK CHAIR, 1993
upholstery and wood
37½ x 40 x 40 inches
collection of Steven Jensen, Los Angeles

THREE LEG STOOL, 1993
cast iron
10½ x 10 x 10 inches
collection of Mr. and Mrs. Fred Arbegast, Los Angeles

DAN COFFEE TABLE, 1996
oak
16 x 72 x 72 inches
collection of Cecilia and Michael Dan

DAN MOROCCAN SIDE TABLE, 1996
found table, paint, and wood
22 x 27 x 27 inches
collection of Cecilia and Michael Dan

ALPHABET SKETCHES, 1997
painted wood
143 works; dimensions variable
courtesy of the artist, Seattle

GETTY MUSEUM OFFICE SIDE TABLE, 1997
Big Leaf maple
25 x 20 x 20 inches
J. Paul Getty Museum, Los Angeles

HALL TABLE, 1997
painted wood and glass
32¾ x 32 x 22⅜ inches
Rhodes Collection, Seattle

UNTITLED (THREE-SHELF CASE, PARTIALLY OPEN), 1997
painted plywood and composite wood
38¾ x 27½ x 10½ inches
courtesy of the artist, Seattle

UNTITLED (UPHOLSTERED OTTOMAN), 1997
wool fabric and painted maple
18 x 27 x 16 inches
collection of the artist, Seattle

UNTITLED (UPHOLSTERED STOOL), 1997
wool upholstery and painted composite wood
26 x 18 x 18 inches
courtesy of the artist, Seattle

KNEW SWIVEL WINGBACK CHAIR, 1998
upholstery, painted wood, and hardware
32 x 36 x 36 inches
courtesy of Domestic Furniture Co., Seattle

I LOVE U SMALL CHEST, 1999
enamel and maple
20 x 30 x 24 inches
collection of Stuart Bloomberg and Mary Farrell, Santa Monica

KNEW DRESSER, 1999
painted eastern maple
55 x 30 x 17 inches
courtesy of Domestic Furniture Co., Seattle

WOULD CHINA CABINET, 1999
walnut and painted maple
two units: 69 x 40 x 21 inches each
collection of Kim Light, Los Angeles

WOULD MODERN CHAIR, 1999
Big Leaf maple
36 x 22 x 19 inches
courtesy of Domestic Furniture Co., Seattle

WOULD SIDE TABLE EXTRA PATCHY, 1999
walnut
20 x 18 x 18 inches
courtesy of Domestic Furniture Co., Seattle

1305 TABLE, 2000
holly
28½ x 26 x 26 inches
Berro Collection, Beverly Hills

FLOOR SCULPTURE, 2000–01
poplar, steel, and enamel
42 x 14 x 14 inches
courtesy of the artist, Seattle

HANGING SCULPTURE, 2000
enamel on wood with metal hardware and ro
42 x 14 x 14 inches
courtesy of the artist, Seattle

LIGHT COFFEE TABLE, 2000
mixed media
17 x 29 x 60 inches
collection of Kim Light, Los Angeles

MARECHAL MACMAHON, 2000
gouache on paper
14 x 11 inches
collection of Cecilia and Michael Dan

PAINTING OF A VANITY, 2000
oil paint on wood panel
36 x 27 x 2¾ inches
courtesy of the artist and Feature Inc., New Y

PETRA/WONG BREAKFAST ROOM SERVER, 2
painted wood
34 x 40 x 20 inches
collection of Tina Petra and Kenneth Wong, Los Angeles

REFRIGERATOR, TABLE, SHELVING UNIT, 20
maple, plywood, and enamel paint; edition I/
70 x 31 x 32 inches
private collection. Courtesy of Feature Inc., New

SCULPTURE WITH DRAWER, 2000
poplar, steel, and enamel
42 x 14 x 14 inches
collection of Stuart Bloomberg and Mary Farr
Santa Monica

SHELVING UNIT WITH DECORATION AND SHIMS, 2000
enamel paint on wood
60 x 48 x 48 inches
Museum of Contemporary Art, San Diego

TWO CHESTS, ONE WITH NO KNOBS, ONE WITH SLIGHTLY OVERSIZED DRAWERS, 2
plywood, maple, and enamel paint; edition I/
58 x width varies x 20 inches each
private collection, New York

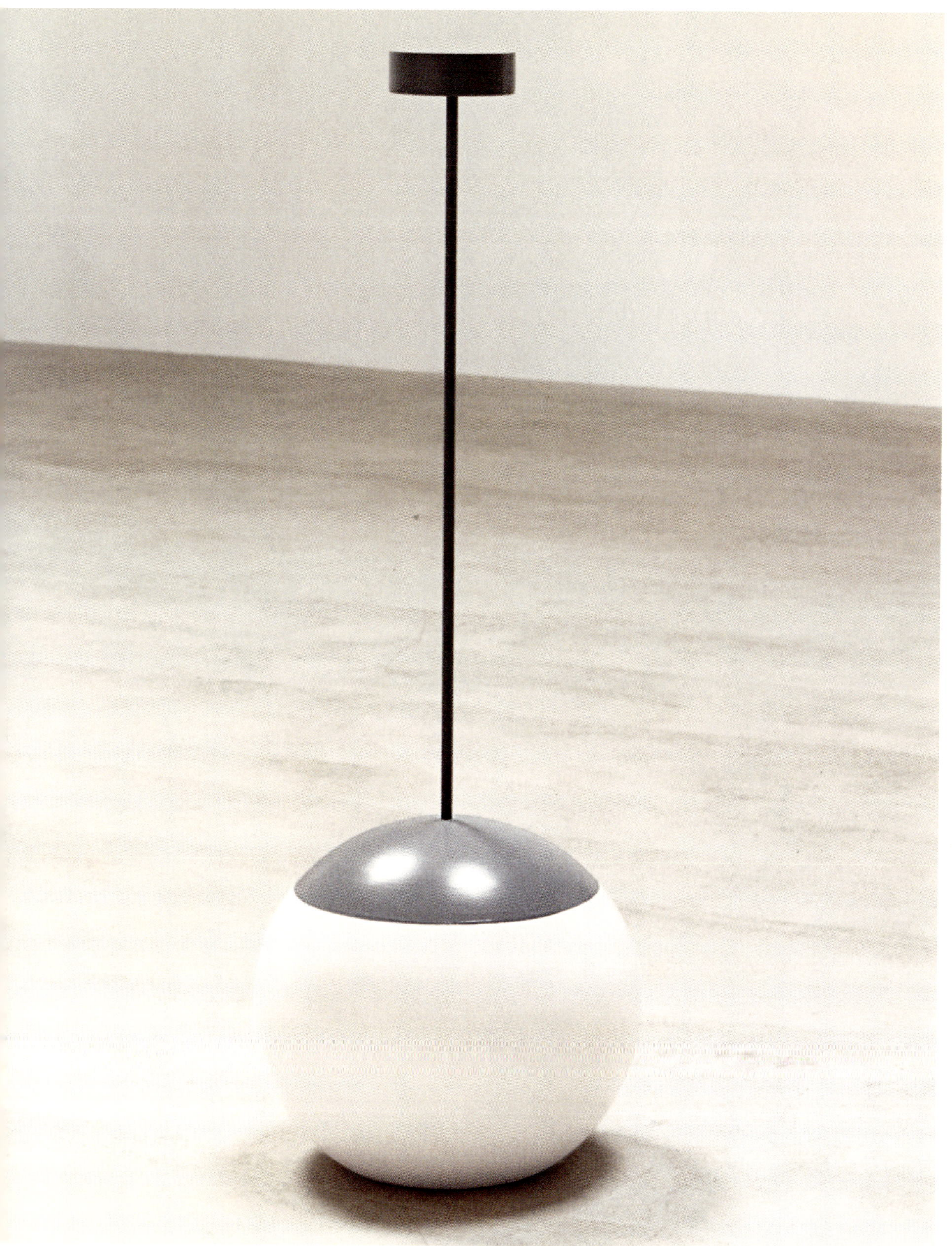

FLOOR SCULPTURE, 2000–01

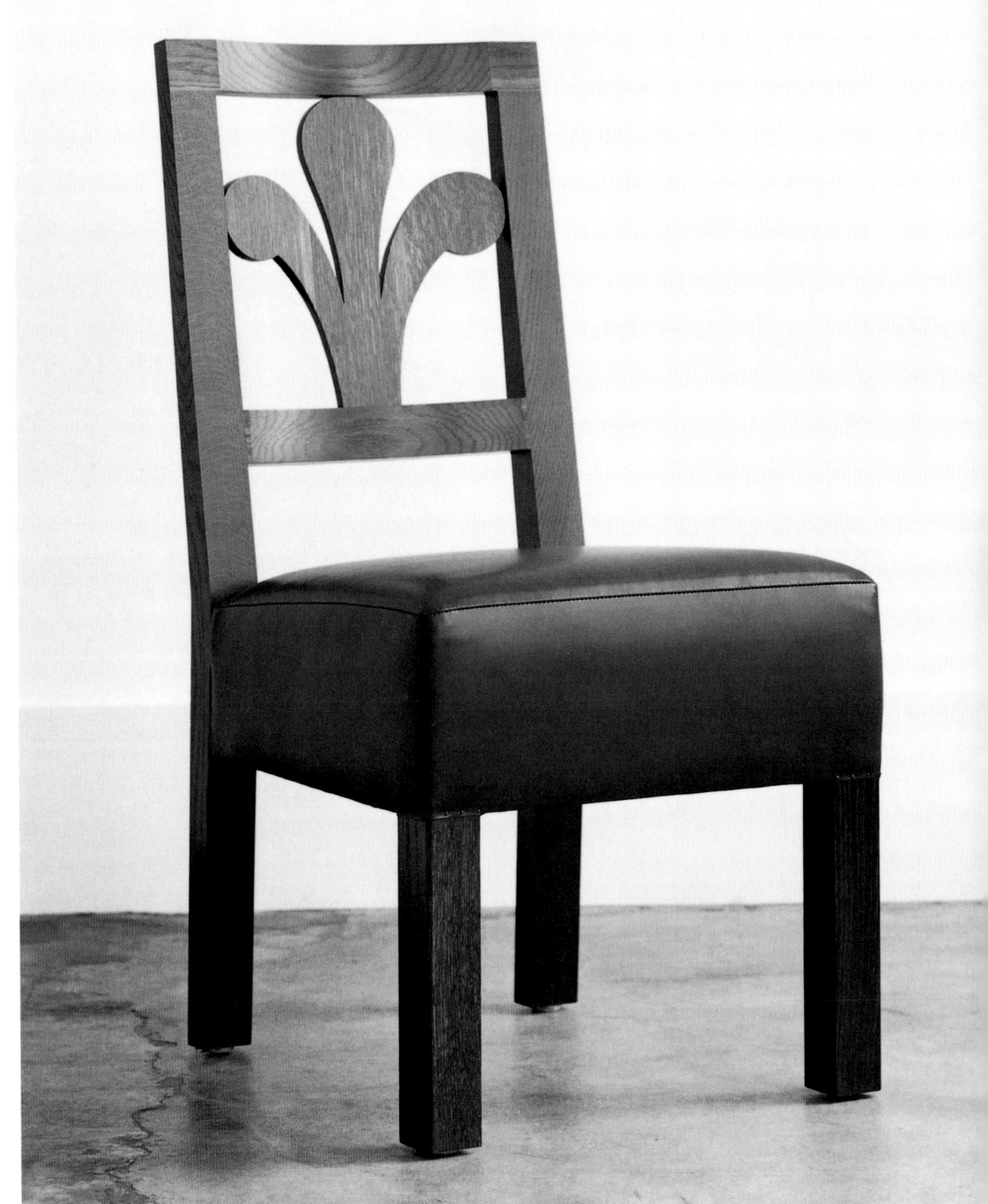

LORENZEN/KOCH DINING CHAIR, 2001

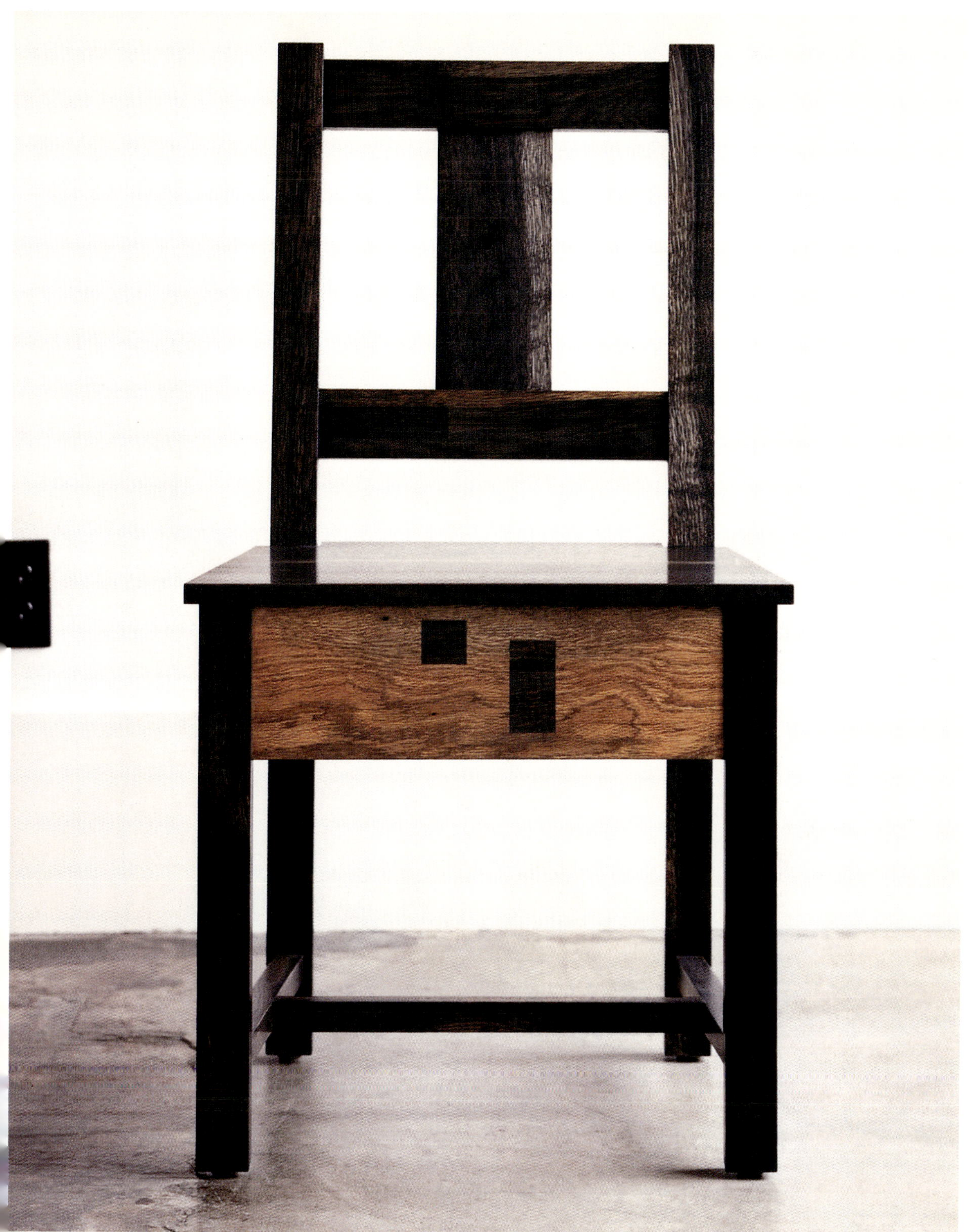

WOULD SIMPLE CHAIR, 2000

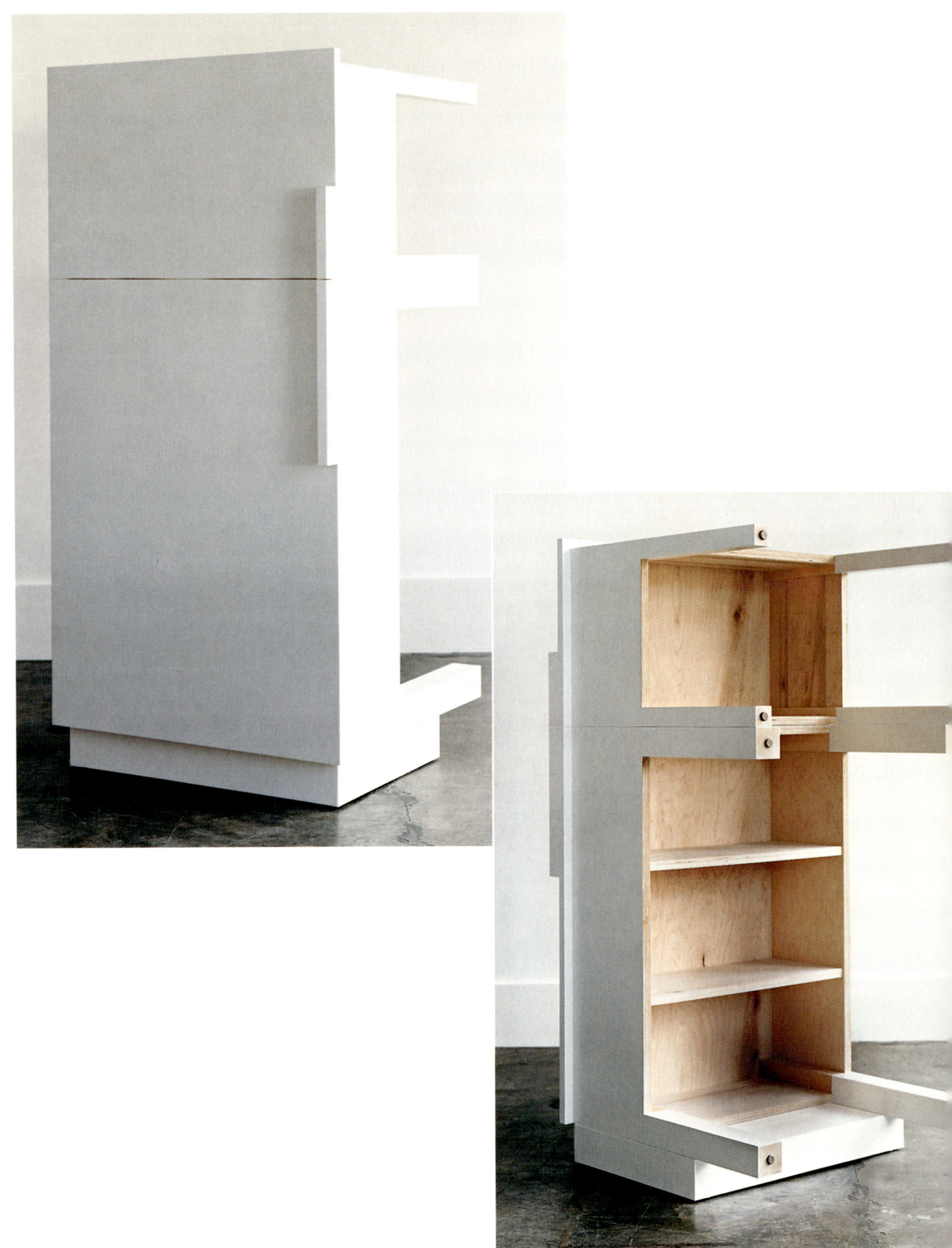

REFRIGERATOR, TABLE, SHELVING UNIT, 2000

WHERE AM I?, 2000
masonite, plastic, pencil, and latex paint
48 x 60 inches
Benedek Collection, Los Angeles

WOULD SIMPLE CHAIR, 2000
ebonized oak
36 x 22 x 19 inches
Berro Collection, Beverly Hills

WRITING TABLE AND CHAIR, 2000
painted wood
29½ x 52 x 24 inches; chair: 36 x 22 x 19 inches
Smith/Clark Collection, Oakland

DAWN'S DESK CHAIR, 2001
holly
38 x 18 x 18 inches
courtesy of Domestic Furniture Co., Seattle

ENAMEL-TOP TABLE, 2001
painted wood and enameled steel
14 x 14 x 14 inches
Lorenzen/Koch Collection, Seattle

GHEZ SIDE TABLE/STOOLS, 2001
painted wood
16 x 19 x 19 inches each
collection of Susanne Ghez, Chicago

LORENZEN/KOCH DINING CHAIR, 2001
ebonized oak and black leather
36 x 19 x 19 inches
Lorenzen/Koch Collection, Seattle

LORENZEN/KOCH SERVER, 2001
ebonized oak
38 x 77 x 19 inches
Lorenzen/Koch Collection, Seattle

CHEST OF DRAWERS, 2001/03
painted wood
56 x 38 x 21 inches
courtesy of Domestic Furniture Co., Seattle

UNTITLED, 2001
enamel paint, wood, and mirror
two chairs; 36 x 22 x 19 inches each
True Collection, Seattle

WOULD FANCY CHAIR, 2001
wood and upholstery
38 x 22 x 19 inches
private collection, Los Angeles

WRIGHT END TABLE, 2001
holly
22 x 18 x 15 inches
collection Robin M. Wright, San Francisco

ANVIL LAMP, 2002
enamel on wood, metal, and electrical hardware
12 x 22 x 10 inches
courtesy of Domestic Furniture Co., Seattle

BENEDEK HOUSE MODEL, 2002
walnut, paint, and mixed media
36 x 40 x 66 inches
Benedek Collection, Los Angeles

UNTITLED, 2002
oil on panel and enamel on wood
dimensions variable
courtesy of Feature Inc., New York

UNTITLED (RUG), 2002
wool
96 x 120 inches
courtesy of Domestic Furniture Co., Seattle

WALNUT DRESSER, 2002
walnut
38 x 40 x 19 inches
courtesy of Domestic Furniture Co., Seattle

LEQUITA FAYE MELVIN, 2003
enamel on wood and wool upholstery
dimensions variable
courtesy of the artist, Seattle

MARIAN PAROO'S PORCH, 2003
wood, enamel paint, metal, glass, and hardware
dimensions variable
courtesy of Feature Inc., New York

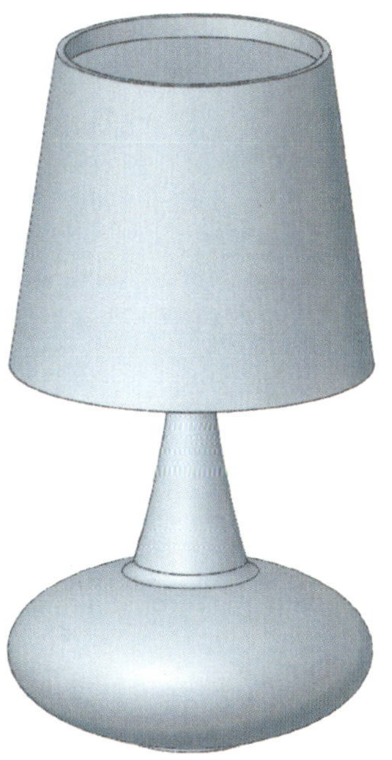

DRAWING OF A LAMP from **LEQUITA FAYE MELVIN,**
2003
computer rendering

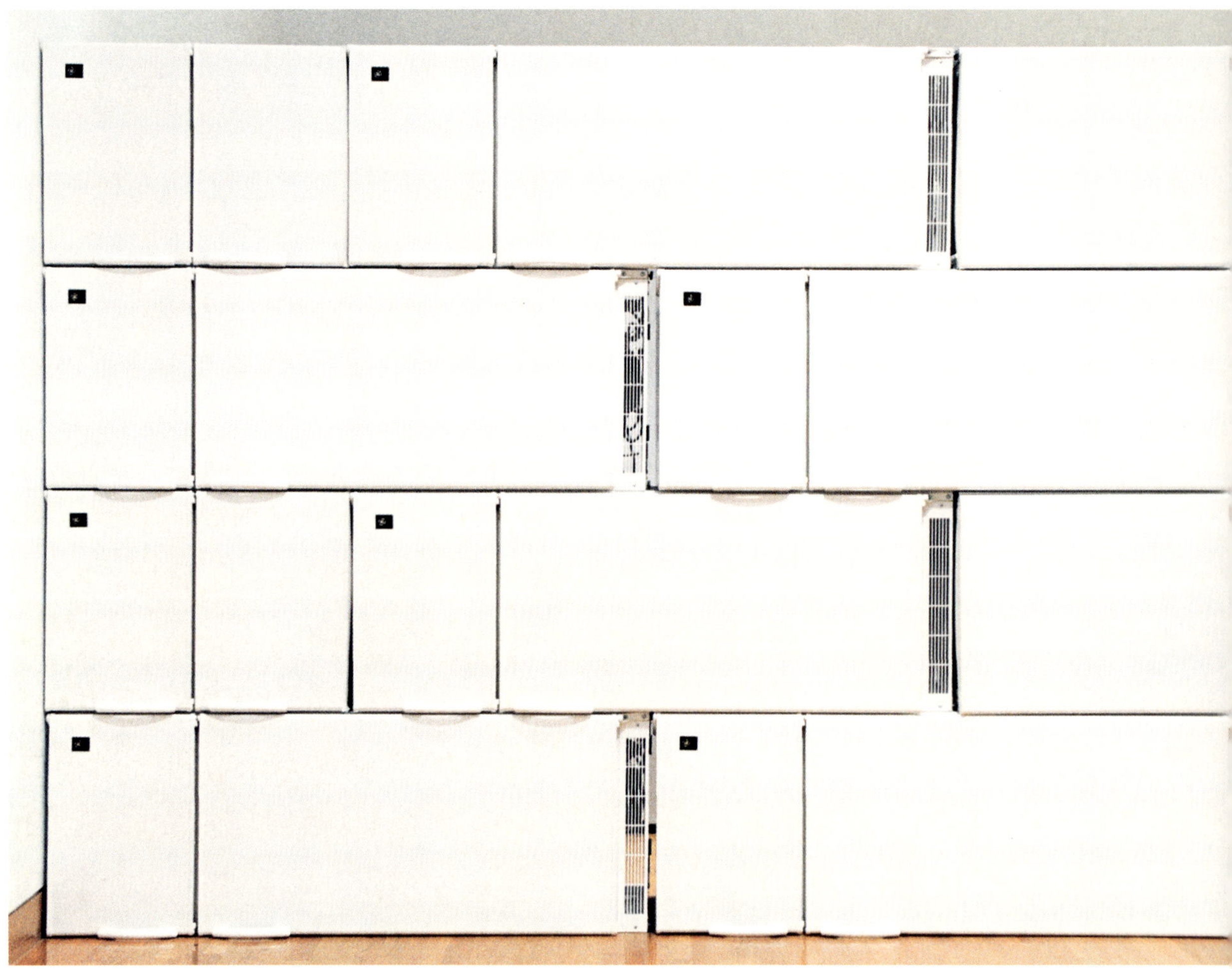

"HOW DO I KNOW HOW YOU KNOW?"
INSTALLATION VIEW, SEATTLE ART MUSEUM, SEATTLE, 1999

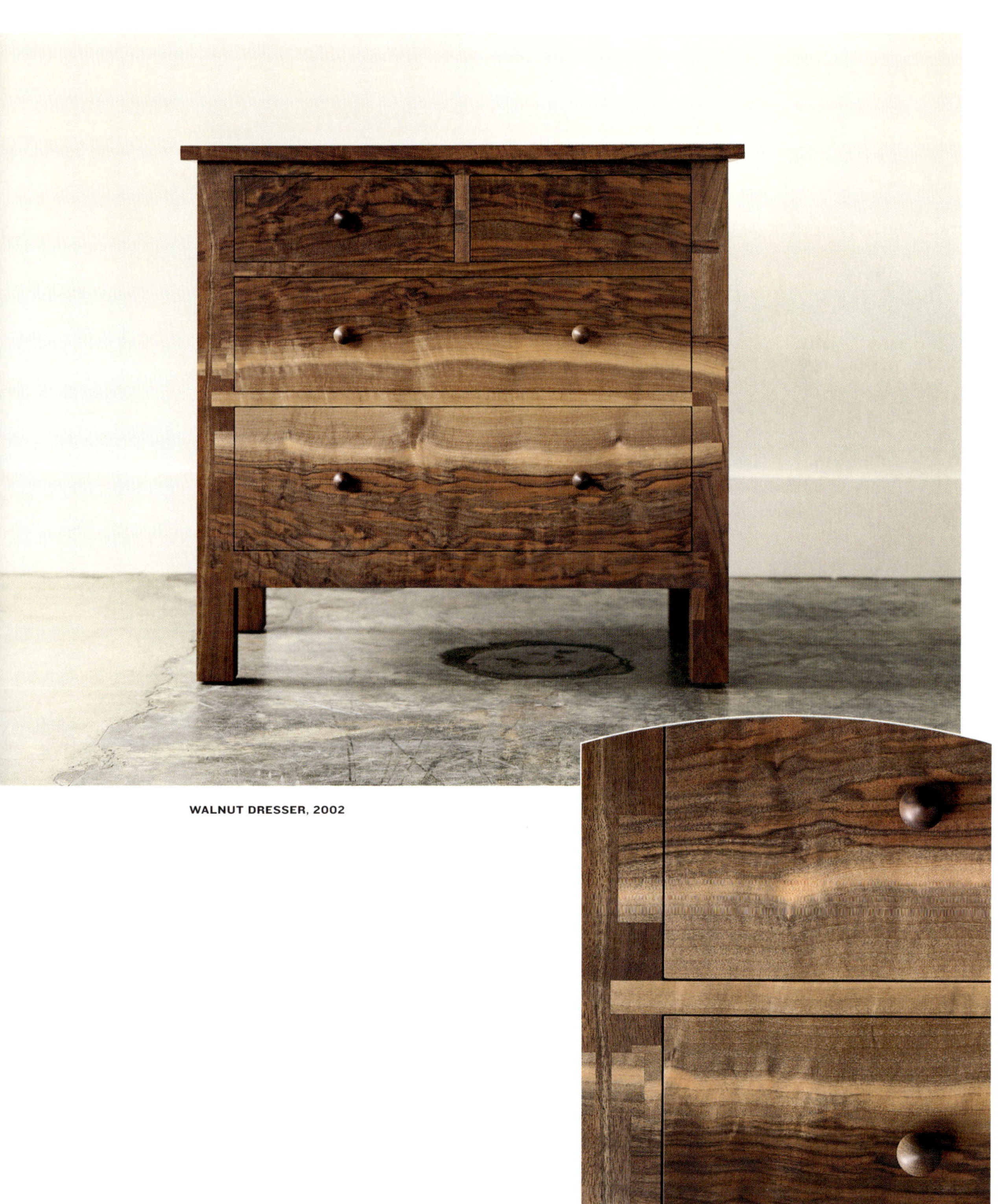

WALNUT DRESSER, 2002

ROY McMAKIN

born in 1956 in Lander, Wyoming
lives and works in Seattle

EDUCATION

1982
M.F.A., University of California at San Diego,
La Jolla, California

1979
B.A., University of California at San Diego,
La Jolla, California

1975–77
Portland Museum Art School,
Portland, Oregon

SOLO EXHIBITIONS

2003
"A Door Meant as Adornment,"
The Museum of Contemporary Art, Los Angeles

2001
"Space,"
Feature Inc., New York

"To 2,"
Quint Contemporary Art, La Jolla, California

2000
"When Is a Door a Jar?,"
Marc Foxx, Los Angeles

1999
"How Do I Know How You Know?,"
Seattle Art Museum, Seattle

1997
Marc Foxx, Santa Monica, California

1987
Quint Gallery, San Diego

1986
Quint Gallery, San Diego

1982
"Inside,"
Michael Dunsford Gallery, San Diego

"A House,"
Sushi, San Diego

"Not Home,"
Mandeville Annex Gallery,
University of California at San Diego, La Jolla, California

1981
"Supine in the Arroyo" (performance),
Sushi, San Diego

1980
"Built-Ins" and "Love in a Charles Eames Chair" (performance),
Sushi, San Diego

"Things from or for Somebody's Home,"
Mandeville Annex Gallery,
University of California at San Diego, La Jolla, California

SELECTED GROUP EXHIBITIONS

2001
"Best of the Season:
Highlights from the 2000–'01 Manhattan Exhibition Season,"
Aldrich Museum of Contemporary Art,
Ridgefield, Connecticut

2000
"Against Design,"
Institute of Contemporary Art,
University of Pennsylvania, Philadelphia

"Fast Forward: The Shape of Northwest Design,"
Tacoma Art Museum, Tacoma, Washington

"National Design Triennial: Design Culture Now,"
Cooper-Hewitt National Design Museum,
New York

1999
Feature Inc., New York

"LA CURRENT: The Canvas Is Paper,"
Armand Hammer Museum of Art and Culture Center,
Los Angeles

1998
"YOYOGAGA,"
Feature Inc., New York

1997
Marc Foxx, Santa Monica, California

"Simple Form,"
Henry Art Gallery, Faye G. Allen Center for the Visual Arts,
University of Washington, Seattle

1987
"911: A House Gone Wrong,"
Parameters 8, San Diego, and
La Jolla Museum of Contemporary Art, La Jolla, California

"Selections from the Permanent Collection,"
La Jolla Museum of Contemporary Art, La Jolla, California

1986
"The RMS Collection,"
Cincinnati Art Museum, Cincinnati

1985
"A San Diego Exhibition: 42 Emerging Artists,"
La Jolla Museum of Contemporary Art, La Jolla, California

"To the Astonishing Horizon,"
Los Angeles Visual Arts, Los Angeles

"Wood,"
Quint Gallery, San Diego

1984
"Contextual Furnishings: Isermann, McMakin, Vaughn,"
Mandeville Art Gallery, University of California at San Diego,
La Jolla, California

"Significant Others,"
Patty Aande Gallery, San Diego

"Three from Paris, Three from L.A.,"
Angles Gallery, Santa Monica, California

1982
"Carol Mavor and Roy McMakin,"
Jewish Community Center Gallery, San Diego

SELECTED BIBLIOGRAPHY

Abramovitch, Ingrid. "The Trickster." *House & Garden* 171, no. 2 (February 2002): 74–81.

Against Design. Exh. cat. Philadelphia: Institute of Contemporary Art, University of Pennsylvania, 2000.

Bartolucci, Marisa. "Fate-of-the-Earth Furniture." *Home Design*, part two of *The New York Times Magazine*, 10 October 1993, 11–12.

Bowles, Hamish, ed. "Back to the Future." *Vogue* 184, no. 4 (April 1994): 385–87.

Cotter, Holland. "Roy McMakin at Feature." *The New York Times*, 16 February 2001, E39.

Darling, Michael. "Domesticating Art." *L.A. Weekly*, 19–25 December 1997, 43.

Duncan, Michael. "Live from the Getty." *Art in America* 86, no. 5 (May 1998): 98–101.

Helmers, Glenn. "Glamour Gets a Face-lift in Old Hollywood." *Metropolitan Home* 26, no. 6 (November/December 1994): 108–11.

Landis, Dylan. "The Message Is the Mission." *Metropolitan Home* 25, no. 6 (November/December 1993): 62–67.

National Design Triennial: Design Culture Now. Exh. cat. New York: Cooper-Hewitt National Design Museum, Smithsonian Institution; and New York: Princeton Architectural Press, 2000.

Schwartz, Bonnie. "The *I.D.* Forty: Tapping the Collective Unconscious." *I.D.* 42, no. 1 (January/February 1995): 62–63.

Stein, Karen. "Interview: Roy McMakin." *Architectural Record* 185, no. 9 (September 1997): 118–23.

Viladas, Pilar. "This Is Not a Dresser." *The New York Times Magazine*, 14 January 2001, 39–45.

Webb, Michael. "Domestic Twist." *Los Angeles Times Magazine*, 15 July 2001, 24–30.

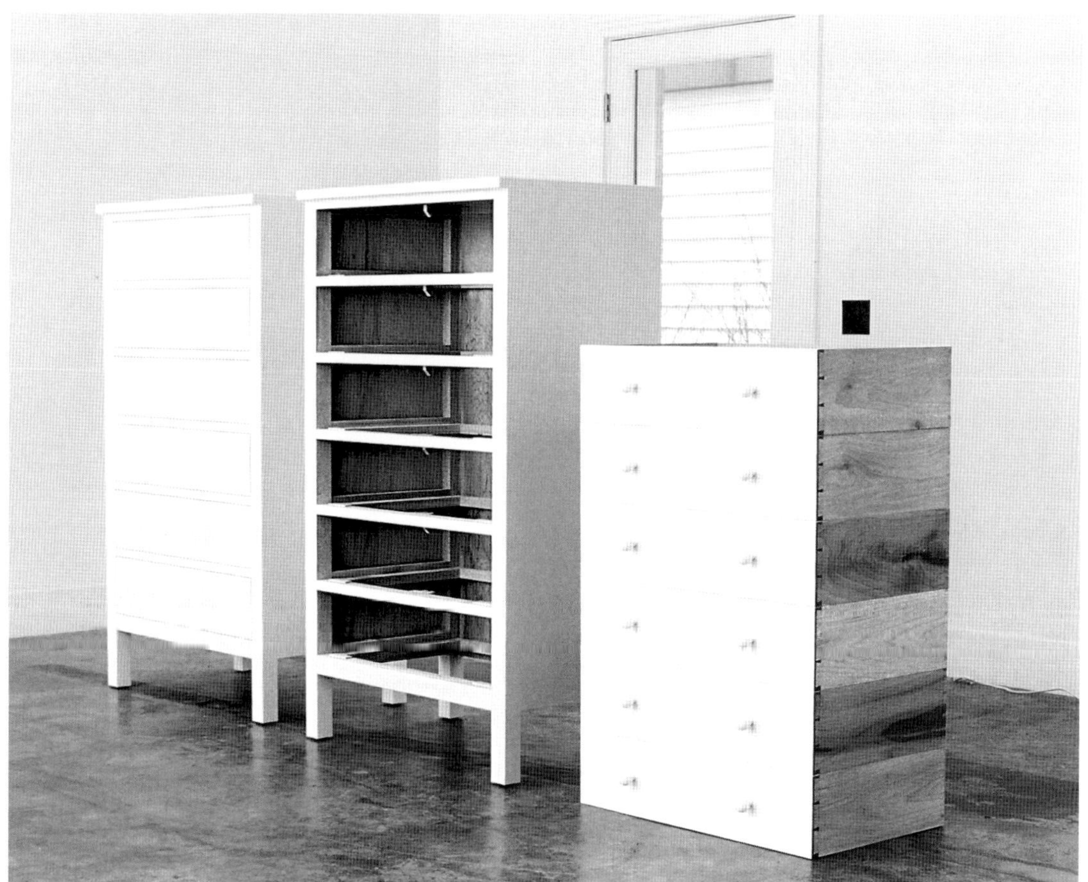

TWO CHESTS, ONE WITH NO KNOBS, ONE WITH SLIGHTLY OVERSIZED DRAWERS, 2000

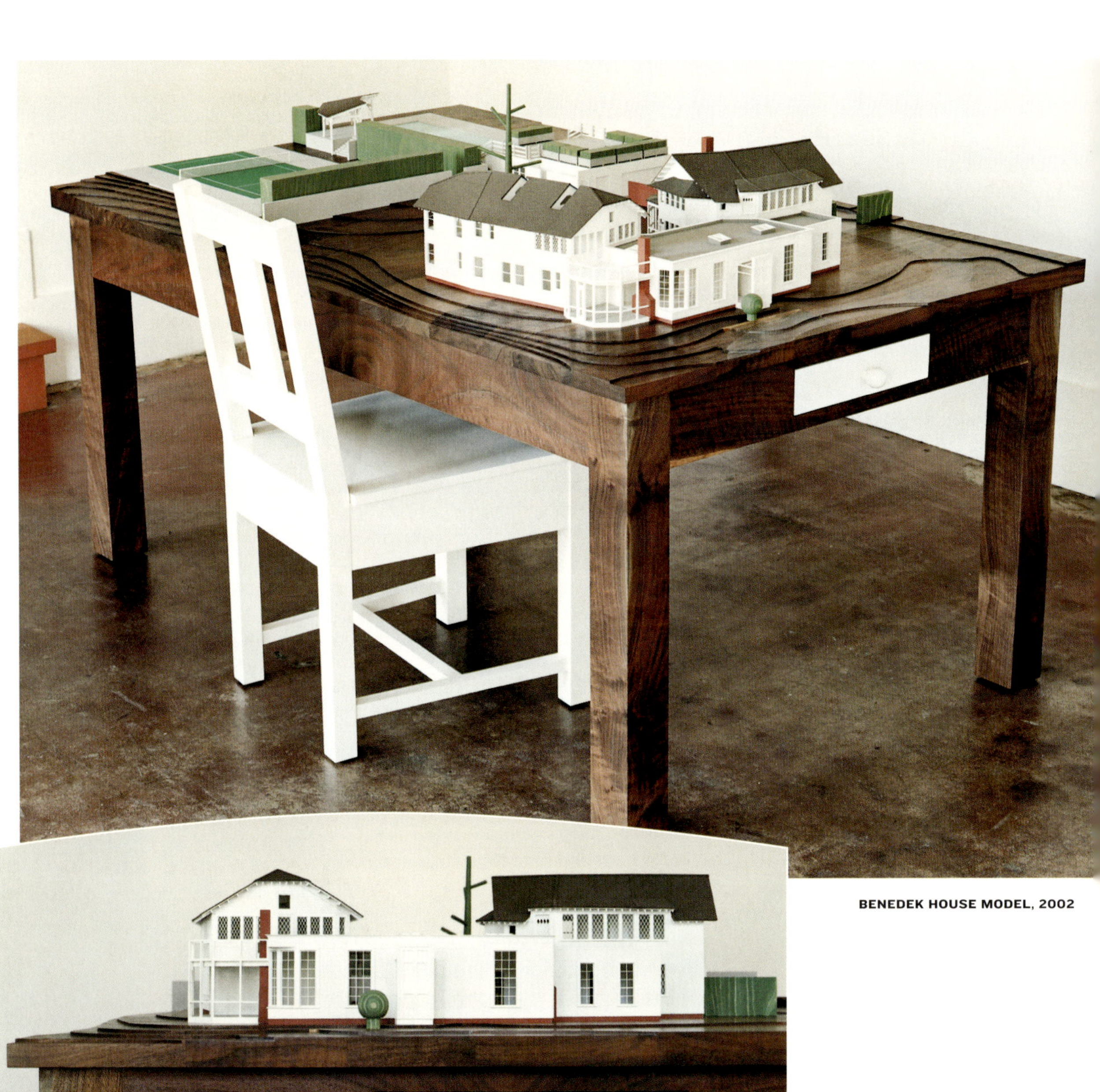

BENEDEK HOUSE MODEL, 2002

SELECTED ARCHITECTURAL, PUBLIC ART, and DESIGN COMMISSIONS

BENEDEK RESIDENCE, 2002–
Southampton, New York
architectural and interior design

BLOOMBERG/FARRELL RESIDENCE 2, 2002–
Mattapoisett, Massachusetts
architectural remodel; interior and furniture design

CAMP STREET PROJECT, 2002
San Antonio, Texas
architectural remodel; interior and furniture design
unrealized

DUFFY RESIDENCE, 2002–
Manhattan Beach, California
architectural and interior design

JONES RESIDENCE, 2002
San Antonio, Texas
architectural remodel; interior and furniture design

PRIVATE ARTS FOUNDATION GALLERY, 2002–
Seattle
architectural remodel

UNIVERSITY OF CALIFORNIA AT SAN FRANCISCO MISSION BAY CAMPUS, 2002–
San Francisco
exterior sculpture and seating

DAWSON PLUMBING, 2001
Seattle
architectural tenant improvement

FLORA & HENRI STORE, 2001
Seattle
architectural tenant improvement;
interior and furniture design

LORENZEN/KOCH RESIDENCE, 2001
Seattle
interior and furniture design

SMITH/CLARK RESIDENCE, 2001
Oakland, California
interior and furniture design

SWOFFORD RESIDENCE, 2001–02
Los Angeles
interior and furniture design

BERRO RESIDENCE, 2000
Beverly Hills, California
architectural remodel; interior and furniture design

FIKSO/FLACK RESIDENCE, 2000
Seattle
architectural remodel; interior and furniture design

LIGHT RESIDENCE, 2000
Larkspur, California
interior and furniture design

MURKOFF RESIDENCE, 2000
Montecito, California
architectural remodel; interior and furniture design

O'HALLORAN RESIDENCE, 2000
Seattle
architectural remodel; interior and furniture design

WRIGHT RESIDENCE, 2000–01
San Francisco
interior and furniture design

BLOOMBERG/FARRELL RESIDENCE, 1999
Santa Monica, California
architectural remodel; interior and furniture design

DENNY BLAINE RESIDENCE, 1999
Seattle
architectural remodel and interior design

YOUNG RESIDENCE, 1999
Chicago
kitchen remodel and furniture design

ABC TELEVISION, 1998
Century City, California
interior and furniture design
for the office of Chairman of Entertainment Division
Stuart Bloomberg

BLOOMBERG/FARRELL RESIDENCE I, 1998
Mattapoisett, Massachusetts
architectural remodel; interior and furniture design

SEA LEVEL, 1998
Venice, California
architectural remodel and addition;
interior and furniture design

J. PAUL GETTY MUSEUM, 1997
Los Angeles
furniture for director's offices, conference rooms,
reception, and study areas

RHODES RESIDENCE, 1997
Seattle
architectural remodel; interior and furniture design
no longer extant

DAN RESIDENCE, 1996
Malibu, California
interior and furniture design

MUSEUM OF CONTEMPORARY ART, SAN DIEGO, 1995
La Jolla, California
furniture design for the office of Director Hugh Davies

SPOT WELDERS PRODUCTIONS, 1994
Venice, California
interior and furniture design

J.CREW, 1992–94
various store locations
design consultant

BENEDEK RESIDENCE, 1989
Brentwood, California
architectural remodel; interior and furniture design

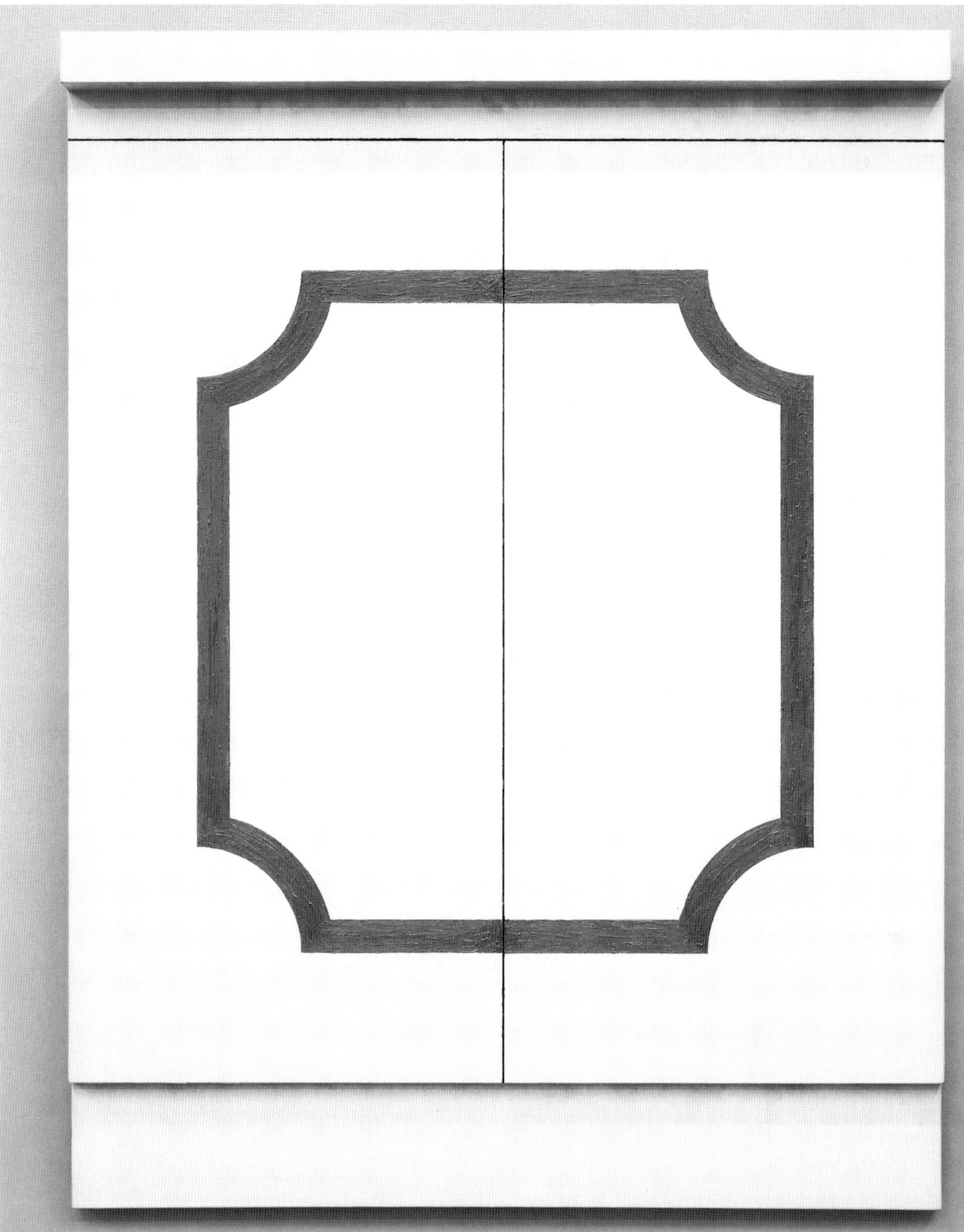

PAINTING OF A VANITY, 2000

AFTERWORD

Roy McMakin is one of the most innovative designers to come out of Los Angeles in the past twenty years. While his highly individual approach to furniture-making has been closely followed by the local art community, his influence is spreading, as evidenced by major commissions in Texas, Washington, and New York and a profusion of national press coverage. McMakin's work is characterized by its humor, beauty, and craftsmanship, as well as its humaneness; it lends itself as easily to daily use as it does to objective contemplation.

McMakin's work does not simply reshape typical modernist furniture and design concepts, but bases its approach to modern design on such idiosyncratic predecessors as Irving Gill, Gerrit Rietveld, George Nakashima, John Woolf, and John McLaughlin. McMakin is also a pioneer in the hybrid genre of art/design, which has become so prevalent since the 1990s in the work of artists such as Jim Isermann, Jorge Pardo, Pae White, Liam Gillick, and Tobias Rehberger. However, McMakin is unique in developing two distinct practices: one purely devoted to serving functional needs in design, the other comprising emphatically non-functional artworks.

The Museum of Contemporary Art, Los Angeles, is thrilled to mount this exhibition, as it is representative of our expanded mandate to document the most exciting developments in design. We're especially proud to focus on someone whose early history is enmeshed in the history and culture of Southern California. Michael Darling's insightful essay and attentively curated exhibition allow us to consider where McMakin's work is situated in sensibility as an artist and as a designer.

Exhibitions such as this require the support of visionary trustees and sponsors, and Audrey Irmas is both. I am truly grateful for her support. In addition, I'd like to thank House and Garden, The Ron Burkle Endowment for Architecture and Design Programs, the Pacific Design Center, Electrolux Home Products, Fine Paints of Europe, and Robin M. Wright for their generosity towards this exhibition.

Finally I would like to express my gratitude to Roy McMakin, a remarkable innovator and a dedicated craftsman. His commitment to this exhibition has enhanced it immeasurably.

JEREMY STRICK
Director
The Museum of Contemporary Art
Los Angeles

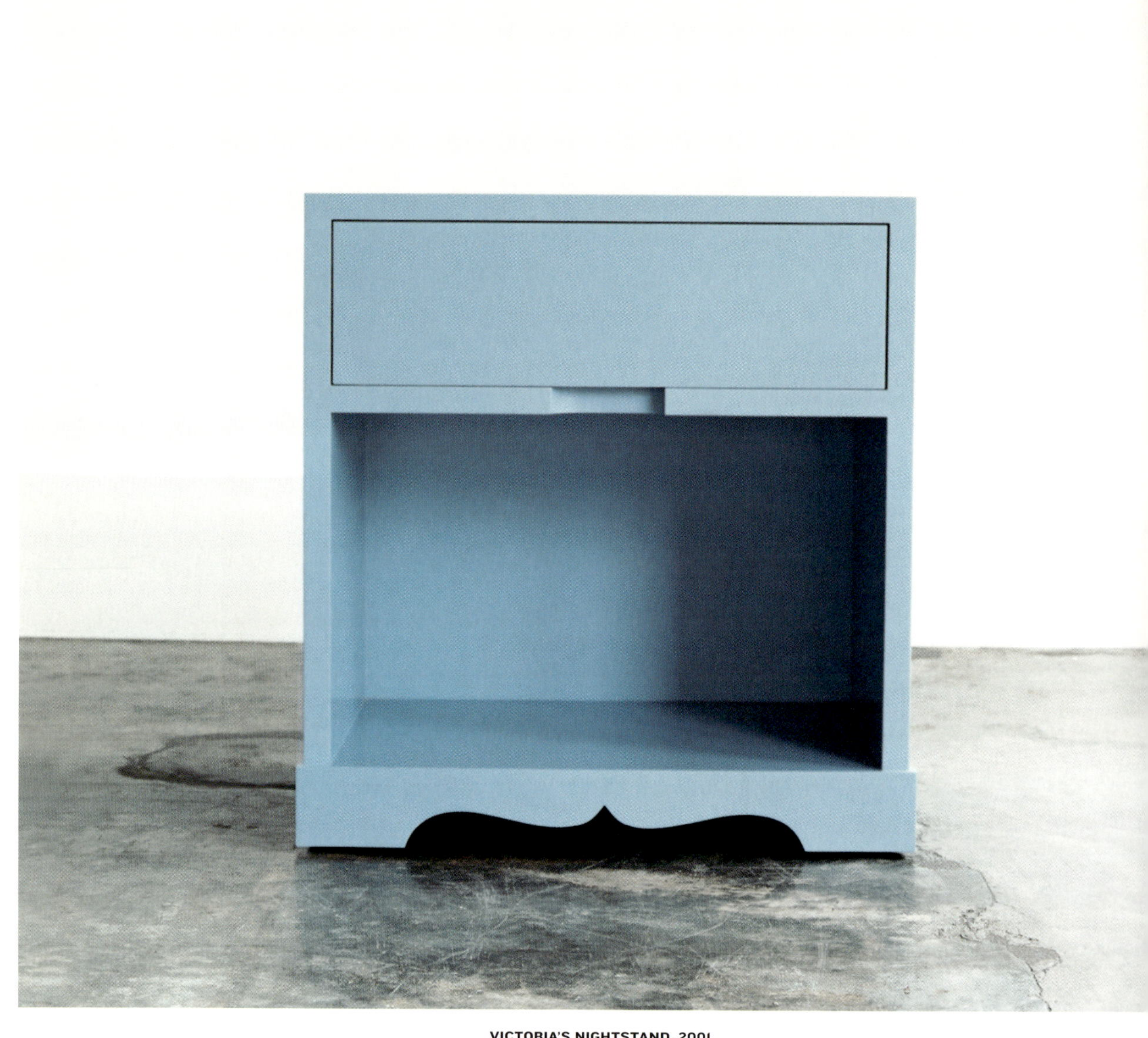

VICTORIA'S NIGHTSTAND, 2001
painted eastern maple
24 x 22 x 16 inches

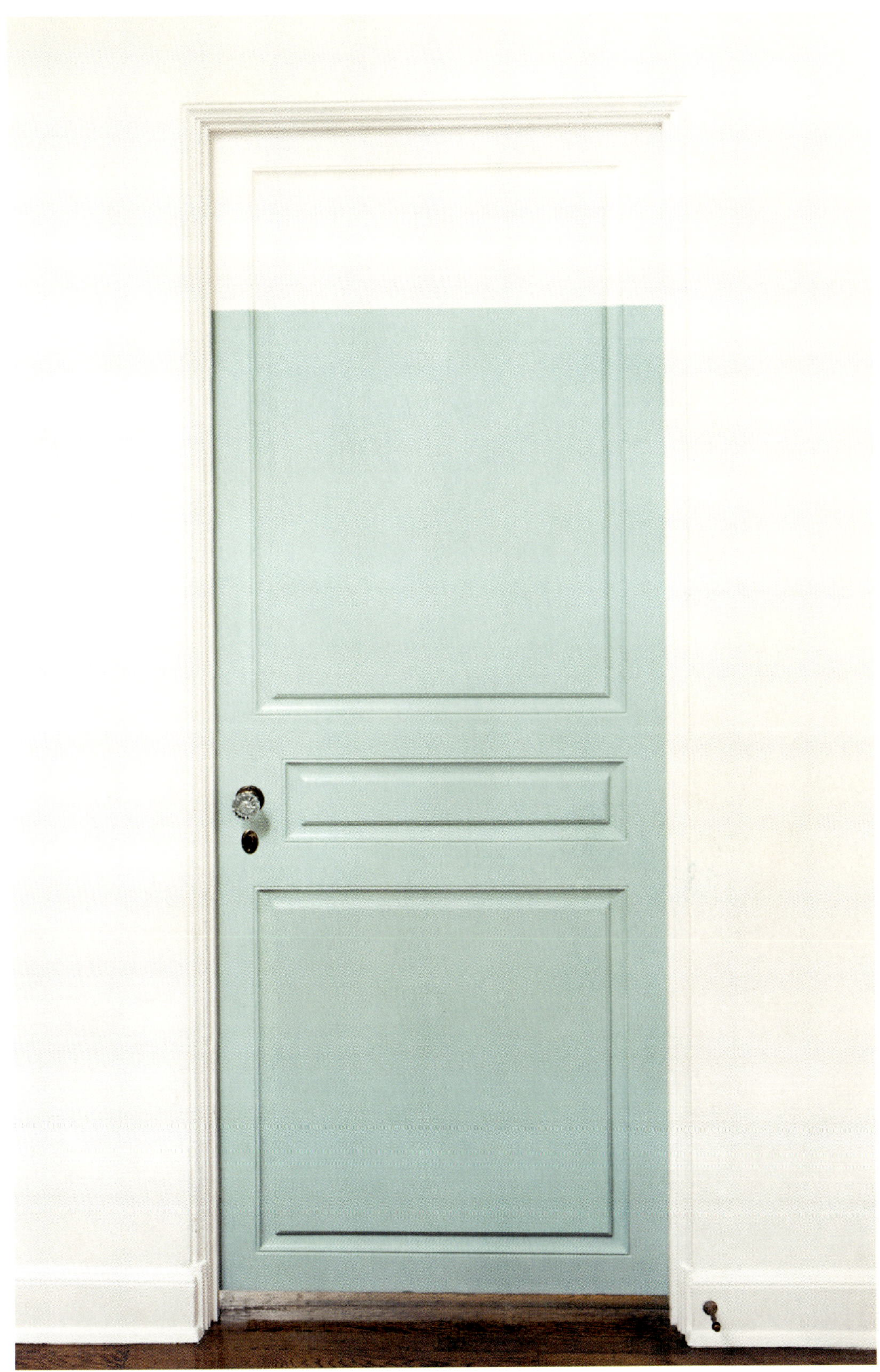

RHODES RESIDENCE, SEATTLE, 1997
no longer extant

ACKNOWLEDGMENTS

A publication and exhibition devoted to surveying the incredibly diverse career of Roy McMakin is long overdue. Over the past twenty years Roy has established himself as one of the premier furniture designers in the country. His list of admirers is long and growing, though the fascinating intricacies of his development have only been known to a few very close friends and followers. It is hoped that this book and exhibition show Roy to be a pioneer in the marriage of design and art (which gained such momentum in the 1990s), a wholly original interpreter of Southern California design history, and the author of a witty, sensible, sensual, and memory-laden language of furniture forms.

There are numerous individuals who have been instrumental in the success of this endeavor, foremost among them Audrey M. Irmas, whose early financial commitment to the show ensured its realization at The Museum of Contemporary Art, Los Angeles (MOCA). Director Jeremy Strick and Chief Curator Paul Schimmel have also been enthusiastic supporters of the project from the beginning, recognizing the continuing importance of Roy's work to the Los Angeles cultural community. Director Richard Andrews and Chief Curator Elizabeth Brown at the Henry Art Gallery in Seattle have also been important partners in this exhibition, heralding Roy's artistry in the city he now calls home.

MOCA has often turned to the immensely talented graphic designer Lorraine Wild to produce beautiful, lasting publications, and we are honored that she rose to the occasion once again. Her sensitivity to Roy's work, having followed it for many years, has resulted in a book that captures its sublime subtlety and lives up to his exacting standards. A similar standard has been set forth by MOCA's editorial staff under the leadership of Senior Editor Lisa Mark who, with Editor Jane Hyun and Assistant Editor Elizabeth Hamilton, kept this publication on track through each and every phase of production, while Jessica Fleischmann in Lorraine's office was also a tireless contributor to the project. Curatorial Assistants Rebecca Morse and Tami Simonian were indispensable colleagues, carefully overseeing the myriad tasks required in the making of an exhibition and publication. Editorial input from the artist and a wide circle of his friends and associates has helped to piece together facts and calibrate emphasis, which immeasurably improved the final text.

The exhibition at MOCA has many generous lenders who have in many cases parted with integral components of their domestic spheres in order to tell the story of Roy McMakin and Domestic Furniture Co. For this, we wish to thank Mr. and Mrs. Fred Arbegast; the Benedek family; Alan and Jodie Berro; Stuart Bloomberg and Mary Farrell; Cecilia and

Michael Dan; the J. Paul Getty Museum; Susanne Ghez; Hudson and Feature Inc.; Steven Jensen; Kim Light; the Lorenzen/Koch family; Kelly and Pam McMakin; the Museum of Contemporary Art, San Diego; Anne and Robert Nugent; Elvi Olesen; Tina Petra and Ken Wong; Lee Rhodes; the Rosenberg family; Elaine Smith and Jeff Clark; Spot Welders; Mark Trilling; Bill and Ruth True; Robin M. Wright; four private collectors; and Roy McMakin and Domestic Furniture Co. Marc Foxx was incredibly helpful in locating work and pertinent information about it, while Mark and Anna Quint, Hugh Davies, and Mike Jacobs have shared important stories as well. Hudson has also been a bulwark of support in a number of different ways. The great photography and cooperation of Mark Woods has ensured a lasting record of Roy's creativity, while Philipp Scholz Ritterman and Kurt Helfrich also provided important pictures. The amazing team that Roy has assembled as part of Domestic Furniture Co., Domestic Architecture Co., and Big Leaf Manufacturing have been instrumental in all parts of the exhibition's organization, from gathering and clarifying information to creating drawings for construction elements, overseeing shipping arrangements, and ultimately producing the furniture. The leadership taken by Erik Aasen and Mau Raynor cannot be overestimated, while Jim Brown, Chris Fast, Candice Feldman, Scott Graczyk, Brody James, and Barbara Marino were also extremely helpful.

All of the work arrived safely and efficiently due to the efforts of registrars Rosanna Hemerick and Amy Carlile and was installed with utter professionalism and sensitivity by Brian Gray, Jang Park, Zazu Faure, David Bradshaw, Barry Grady, Valerie West, Monica Gonzalez, Annabelle Medina, and a great crew of part-time installers. The enthusiasm and support of MOCA's curatorial department was also much appreciated throughout the development of this project, and thanks are due to Ann Goldstein, Connie Butler, Brooke Hodge, Alma Ruiz, Stacia Payne, Lynda Bunting, Julia Langlotz, Virginia Edwards, and Beth Rosenblum. Vigorous fundraising efforts by MOCA's development department, including Paul Johnson, Karen Lofgren, and Stephanie Graham, also ensured the realization of this project.

Working closely with Roy has put me in awe of his intelligence, passion, humanity, and humor. The quality of his work combined with his professionalism and dedication made the organization of this project a pleasure from start to finish.

MICHAEL DARLING
Assistant Curator
The Museum of Contemporary Art
Los Angeles

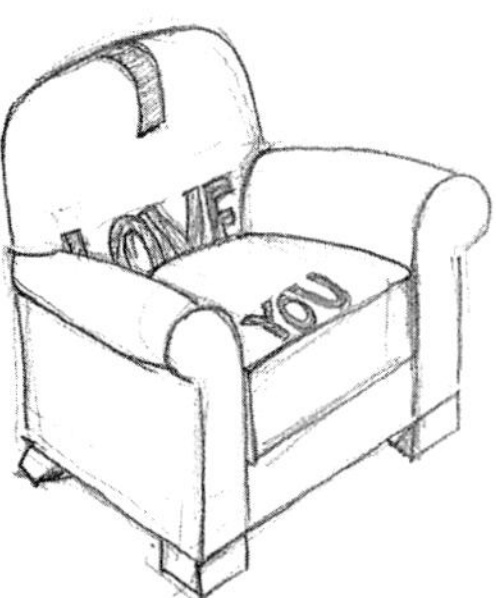

This publication accompanies the exhibition
"ROY McMAKIN: A DOOR MEANT AS ADORNMENT,"
organized by Michael Darling and presented at
THE MUSEUM OF CONTEMPORARY ART, LOS ANGELES
23 March–29 June 2003; and
HENRY ART GALLERY – FAYE G. ALLEN CENTER FOR THE VISUAL ARTS
University of Washington, Seattle
6 February–9 May 2004

"ROY McMAKIN: A DOOR MEANT AS ADORNMENT,"
is sponsored by HOUSE &GARDEN

Additional generous support has been provided by
The Ron Burkle Endowment for Architecture and Design Programs,
the Pacific Design Center, and Audrey M. Irmas.
In-kind support has been provided by Electrolux Home Products
and Fine Paints of Europe.

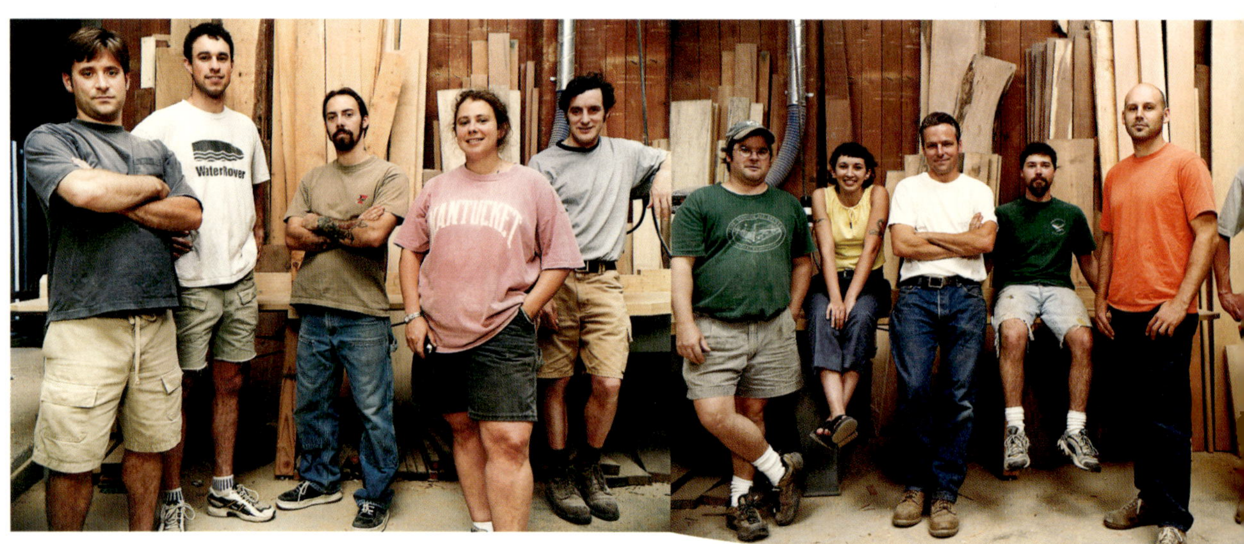

Chris Fast, Damien Farwell, Phrank Barrera, Liz Dryfoos, Geoff Wirth, Tom Young, Mindy Buchheit, Erik Aasen, Frank Peck, Brody James, S

BIG LEAF MANUFACTURING CO., 2001

front cover:
ALPHABET SKETCHES, 1997, detail

frontispiece and page 96:
RHODES RESIDENCE, SEATTLE, 1997
no longer extant

opposite page 1:
HAPPY THOUGHT, 2000
gouache on paper
14 x 11 inches
Benedek Collection, Los Angeles

pages 44–45:
UNTITLED (SKETCHES FOR SCULPTURE), 1996
graphite on paper
11 x 14 inches

pages 60–61:
UNTITLED (SKETCHES FOR A HOUSE), 1996–97
graphite on paper
11 x 14 inches

page 93:
from **UNTITLED (SKETCHES FOR SCULPTU**
graphite on paper
11 x 14 inches

Senior Editor: **LISA MARK**
Editor: **JANE HYUN**
Assistant Editor: **ELIZABETH HAMILTON**
Designers: **LORRAINE WILD** with **JESSICA FLEISCHMANN**
Printer: **DR. CANTZ'SCHE DRUCKEREI, OSTFILDERN, GERMANY**

available through D.A.P./Distributed Art Publishers
155 Sixth Avenue, 2nd Floor, New York, NY 10013
tel: (212) 627-1999 fax: (212) 627-9484

printed and bound in Germany

PHOTO CREDITS

All photographs appear courtesy of the artist and
omestic Furniture Co., Seattle. The following list, keyed to page
numbers, applies to photographs for which
a separate acknowledgment is due:
Mark Woods, pp. front and back covers, 2, 7 bottom right,
42, 44–45, 51–64, 67–74, 78–80, 83–96;
Philipp Scholz Rittermann, pp. 10, 13–15, 30–31;
courtesy of University Art Museum, UCSB, p. 12;
Jason Schmidt, p. 65;
Roe Ethridge, pp. 94–95;
and Roy McMakin, back endsheet.

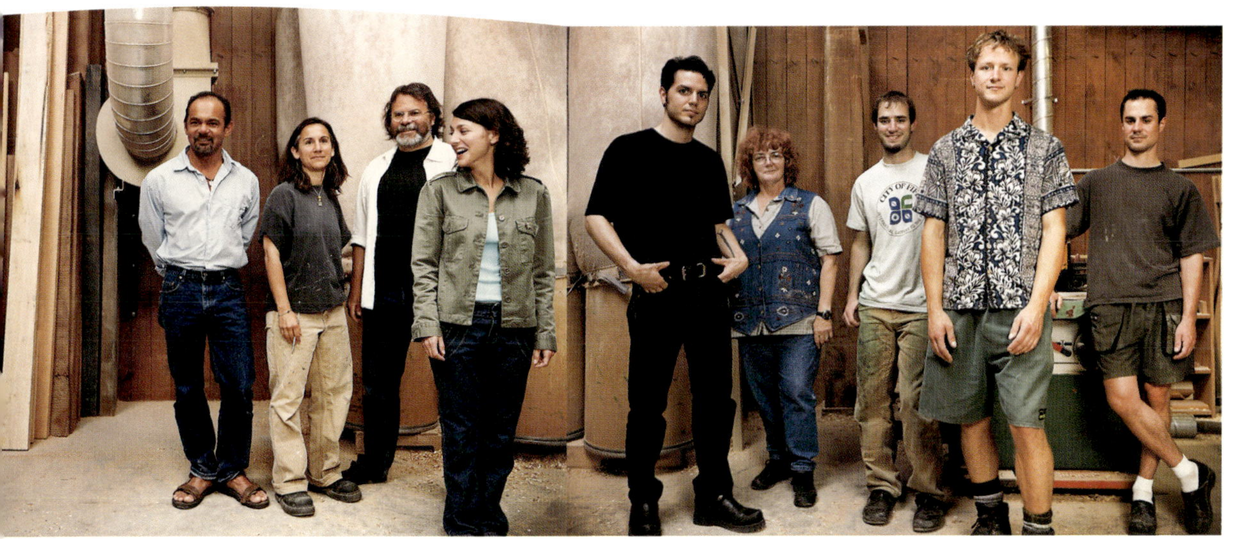

Jim Javelosa, Barbara Marino, Roy McMakin, Candice Feldman, Alex Pursel, Carol Barber, Darren Foote, Carl Beery, John Conoley

ISBN 0-914357-84-0

LIBRARY OF CONGRESS CATALOGING-IN-PUBLICATION DATA
McMakin, Roy, 1956
Roy McMakin: a door meant as adornment /
organized by Michael Darling.
p. cm.

Published to accompany an exhibition held at
the Museum of Contemporary Art,
Los Angeles, Mar. 23–June 29, 2003.
Includes bibliographical references.
ISBN 0-914357-84-0
1. McMakin, Roy, 1956—Exhibitions. I. Darling, Michael.
II. Museum of Contemporary Art (Los Angeles, Calif.) III. Title.

N6537.M31364 A4 2003
749.213—dc21

2002026554

back endsheet:
Roy McMakin's desk, Seattle, 2002
sculpture by Jeffry Mitchell

opposite page 96:
GOBLIN, 2000
gouache on paper
14 x 11 inches
k Collection, Los Angeles

back cover:
JONES SIMPLE CHAIR, 2001, detail
long leaf pine
38 x 21 x 19 inches

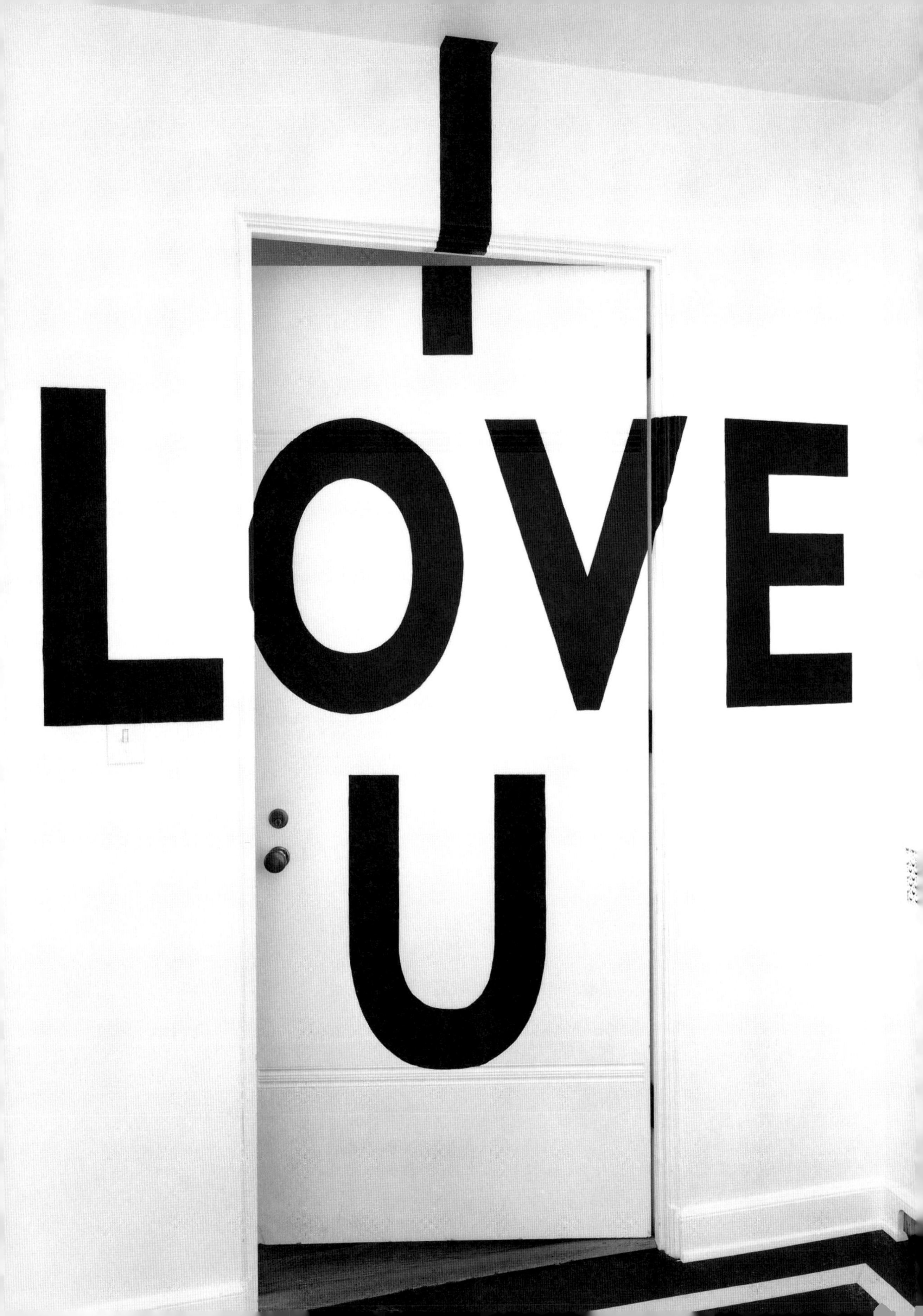

I
LOVE
U

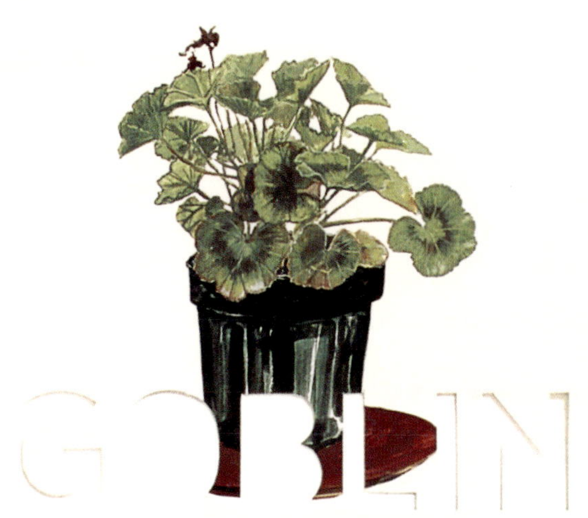
GOBLIN

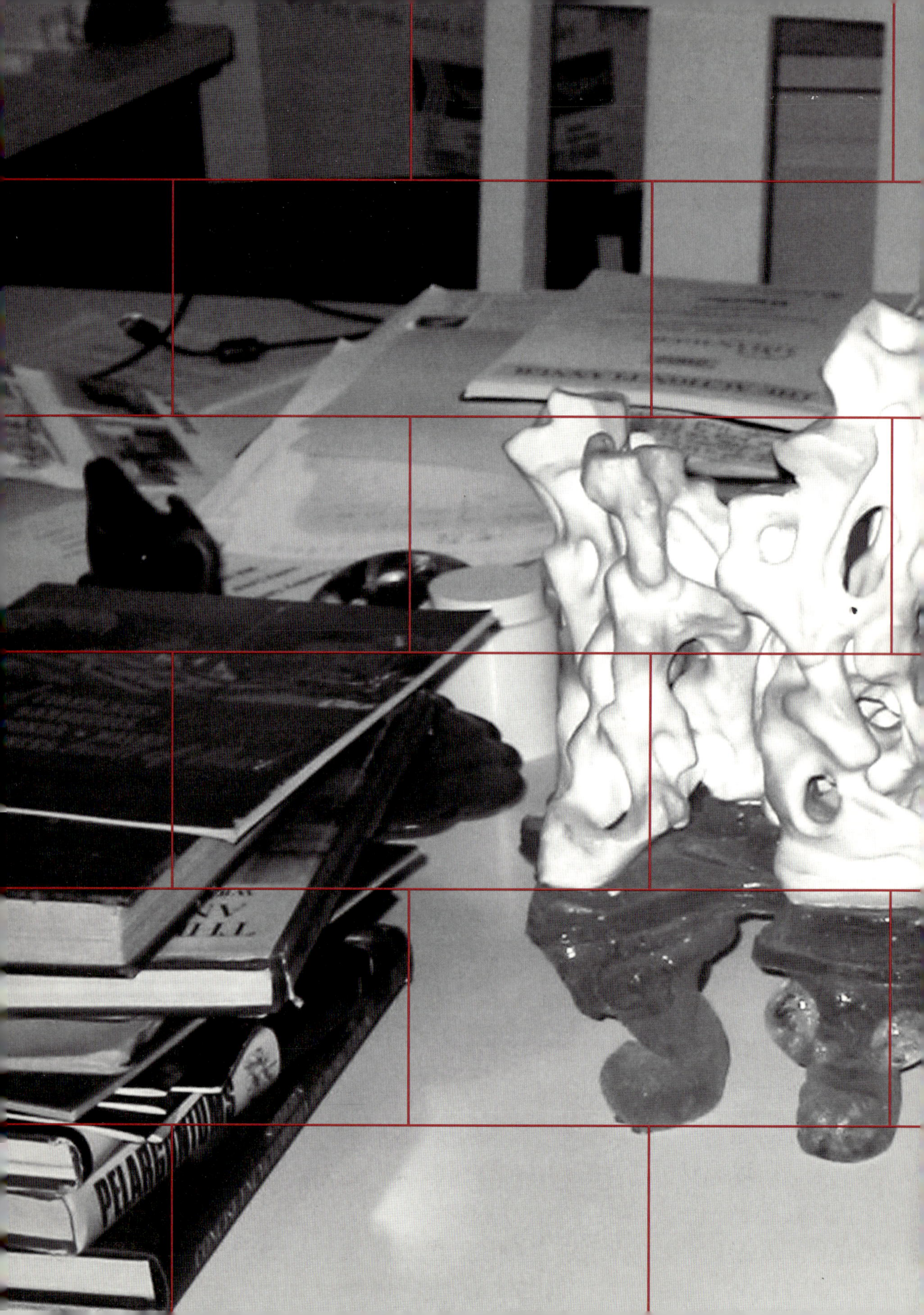